Writing Between Languages

Writing Between Languages

How English Language Learners Make the Transition to Fluency, Grades 4–12

Danling Fu

HEINEMANN
Portsmouth, NH

Heinemann
361 Hanover Street
Portsmouth, NH 03801–3912
www.heinemann.com

Offices and agents throughout the world

Library of Congress Cataloging-in-Publication Data
Fu, Danling.
    Writing between languages : how English language learners make the transition to fluency, grades 4–12 / Danling Fu.
        p.   cm.
    Includes bibliographical references and index.
    ISBN-13: 978-0-325-01395-4
    ISBN-10: 0-325-01395-0
    1. English language—Study and teaching—Foreign speakers.   2. English language—Composition and exercises—Study and teaching.   3. Language arts. 4. Language acquisition.   I. Title.
        PE1128.A2F85   2009
        428.2'4—dc22   2009017422

Editor: Tom Newkirk
Production: Elizabeth Valway
Cover design: Jenny Jensen Greenleaf
Composition: Cape Cod Compositors, Inc.
Manufacturing: Steve Bernier

Printed in the United States of America on acid-free paper
13 12   ML   2 3 4 5

To Donald Graves, a great writing teacher and researcher,
who taught me to observe and listen carefully to children,
and let them teach us how to teach them.

Contents

Foreword

Writing *Between Languages* presents a rich and compelling account of the struggles and accomplishments of newly arrived ELL students as they grapple with the complexities of written English. For most ELL students, writing represents the most challenging language skill to acquire to native-like levels because it demands use of vocabulary, grammatical structures, and rhetorical conventions that are very different from conversational language. Typically, students get relatively little opportunity in classrooms to engage with the creation of meaning through written language. As Danling Fu points out, much of the "writing" that ELL students carry out consists of little more than fill-in-the-blanks exercises or short responses to questions about academic content. One of the reasons for this poverty of writing experience is the perception by many teachers that ELL students must first learn English before they can write in English.

This book makes the claim, which many teachers may find startling, that we have made the development of strong writing skills much more difficult than it needs to be for ELL students in the junior grades and beyond because we have ignored the power of students' first-language (L1) writing skills as a stepping stone to English. Students' L1 represents a potent cognitive tool that they have used up to this point to make sense of their worlds and to acquire new knowledge. There is virtual consensus among cognitive psychologists and reading theorists that students' prior knowledge is the foundation upon which new learning is built (Bransford, Brown, and Cocking 2000). If recently arrived ELL students' prior knowledge is encoded in their L1, then their L1 skills are clearly relevant to their learning of L2.

The research on academic development in two or more languages also highlights the interdependence between languages (Cummins 2001). L1 and L2 academic skills are not separate or isolated from each other; rather they are manifestations of a common underlying proficiency that can be developed by means of input in either language.

The centrality of prior knowledge to all learning and the interdependence of academic skills across languages imply that we should be teaching for transfer across languages rather than creating artificial "English-only" zones in our classrooms. Our own work with ELL students (Cummins et al. 2005) has demonstrated the powerful pedagogical impact of adopting *bilingual instructional strategies* rather than exclusive reliance on monolingual instructional strategies. Madiha, for example, a recently arrived seventh-grade student in Lisa Leoni's class in the Greater Toronto Area worked with two of her Urdu-speaking friends who had been in Canada for several years to write a 20-page bilingual book entitled "The New Country." The story drew on the students' own experiences of immigrating from Pakistan to Canada and was published on the project website (www.multiliteracies.ca). Madiha reflects insightfully about the transfer of academic skills across languages:

> I think it helps my learning to be able to write in both languages because if I'm writing English and Ms. Leoni says you can write Urdu too it helps me think of what the word means because I always think in Urdu. That helps me write better in English. When I came here I didn't know any English, I always speak Urdu to my friends. Other teachers they said to me "Speak English, speak English" but Ms. Leoni didn't say anything when she heard me speak Urdu and I liked this because if I don't know English, what can I do? It helps me a lot to be able to speak Urdu and English.

The rationale for adopting bilingual instructional strategies in the teaching of writing as well as in the teaching of other linguistic and academic skills includes the following research-based considerations:

- Translation skill is widely found among bilingual children by late elementary school (Malakoff and Hakuta 1991; Orellana, Reynolds, Dorner, and Meza 2003). Malakoff and Hakuta highlight potential pedagogical applications, noting that "[t]ranslation provides an easy avenue to enhance linguistic awareness and pride in bilingualism, particularly for minority bilingual children whose home language is not valued by the majority culture" (163).

- For languages such as English and Spanish that have many cognate connections, a focus on cognates can enhance students' knowledge of L2 vocabulary (Nagy, García, Durgunoglu, and Hancin-Bhatt 1993).

- Encouraging newcomer students to write in their L1 and, working with peer, community, or instructional resource people, to translate L1 writing into English scaffolds students' output in English and enables them to use higher-order and critical thinking skills much sooner than if English is the only legitimate language of intellectual expression in the classroom (Cummins et al. 2005; Reyes 2001)

- Legitimating students' L1 as a cognitive tool within the classroom challenges the subordinate status of many minority groups and affirms students' identities (Cummins 2001; García 2008).

I believe that we are at the beginning stages of a radical shift in pedagogical assumptions regarding effective instruction for ELL students. For too long the debate centered on the dueling dichotomies of bilingual education versus English-only programs, with ideological considerations frequently playing a greater role in policy development than any research-based analysis. An increasing number of educators are now beginning to explore how bilingual instructional strategies can be incorporated into English-medium classrooms, thereby opening up the pedagogical space in ways that legitimate the intelligence, imagination, and linguistic talents of ELL students. *Writing Between Languages* makes a highly significant contribution to our understanding of what teaching for transfer entails and what it can achieve in the area of ELL students' writing development.

—Jim Cummins

References

Bransford, J. D., A. L. Brown, and R. R. Cocking. 2000. *How People Learn: Brain, Mind, Experience, and School.* Washington, DC: National Academy Press.

Cummins, J. 2001. *Negotiating Identities: Education for Empowerment in a Diverse Society.* 2nd Edition. Los Angeles: California Association for Bilingual Education.

Cummins, J., V. Bismilla, P. Chow, S. Cohen, F. Giampapa, L. Leoni, P. Sandhu, and P. Sastri. 2005. "Affirming Identity in Multilingual Classrooms." *Educational Leadership* 63 (1): 38–43.

García, O. 2008. *Bilingual Education in the 21st Century. A Global Perspective.* Boston: Basil Blackwell.

Malakoff, M. and K. Hakuta. 1991. "Translation Skills and Metalinguistic Awareness in Bilinguals." In *Language Processing in Bilingual Children*, edited by E. Bialystok, 141–66. Cambridge: Cambridge University Press.

Nagy, W. E., G. E. García, A. Durgunoglu, and B. Hancin-Bhatt. 1993. "Spanish-English Bilingual Students' Use of Cognates in English Reading." *Journal of Reading Behaviour* 25: 241–59.

Orellana, M. F., J. Reynolds, L. Dorner, and M. Meza. 2003. "In Other Words: Translating or 'Para-phrasing' as a Family Literacy Practice in Immigrant Households." *Reading Research Quarterly* 38: 12–34.

Reyes, M. de la Luz. 2000. "Unleashing Possibilities: Biliteracy in the Primary Grades." In *The Best for Our Children: Critical Perspectives on Literacy for Latino Students*, edited by M. de la. Luz Reyes and J. Halcón, 96–121. New York: Teachers College Press.

Acknowledgments

This book reflects a decade of collaborative work between me and bilingual/ESL teachers and school and regional administrators in New York City schools from lower Manhattan to the Bronx. I owe a great deal to those teachers who brought their students' work to me and shared their insights into their students as individuals and into their progress as English language learners and writers. My special thanks go to Betty Mui, and many other veteran ESL teachers at Dr. Sun Yat Sen Middle School, who taught me how to assist struggling students in reaching their potential and to systematically help them grow as learners. Without the consistent support and friendship of Alice Young, the principal of Dr. Sun Yat Sen Middle School and later a local superintendent of Region 9, I would not have lasted a decade in the City.

I am especially grateful to Karen Low, an ESL specialist in Region 9 who worked closely with me in the last three years of my work in the City. It was she who proposed, designed, and facilitated the Literacy Initiative for bilingual/ESL teachers in the region. I admire her knowledge, work ethic, commitment, and endless energy. Without her, my work would not have been as effective.

Nancy Shelton, a close friend and colleague, is a loyal reader of my work and was the first editor of this book. No matter how busy she was, she always promptly gave the most constructive feedback to my work.

Tom Newkirk has been my editor for previous books, and is the editor of this book as well. Working with him was like taking writing lessons, and each of his suggestions not only improved this book, but benefited me as a writer. I am grateful to my editorial coordinator, Stephanie Turner, and production editor, Elizabeth Valway, for their prompt pushing, advice, and assistance during the production process.

My international doctoral students (both present and former), Yildiz Turget, Ivy Hsieh, Ji Dhanarattigannon, Takako Ueno, Shihfen Yet, Qing Liu, Soim Shin, and Mintzu Wang, constantly shared with me their insights as both English language learners and ESL teachers. They inspired me with their fresh ideas, updated knowledge, and great passion for learning and teaching. In our community, we are not only sharing our minds, but our hearts and lives.

My family, Xiaodi, Ashley, and Bill, deserve special credit for my work. Their unconditional love, constant support, and always being there for me not only make my life rich and joyful, but also make it possible for me to conquer any challenges in my work and life. They own part of whatever I have accomplished. I am blessed to have them in my life.

Writing Between Languages

My Decade's Work with ELLs

I was never required to write during my years of English study in China, even in college when I majored in English. And later, when I became an English teacher, I never required my students to write in my seven years of teaching except to have them do some translating or sentence making for grammar or spelling exercises. The first time I was required to write was during my one-year study of American literature as a Fulbright Fellow, two years before I came to the United States to pursue my graduate degree. I will never forget how I struggled through each writing assignment; it seemed nothing came out right—word choices, expressions, or even ideas. I could read English quite well: loved O. Henry, Eugene O'Neill, Arthur Miller, and Emily Dickinson and had little problem communicating with others in English. But I had tremendous difficulty writing in English. When I forced myself to think in English, it seemed I could only squeeze out a few forced ideas, which I could tell were too flat or simple. But when I let myself think in Chinese, my writing didn't sound like English.

Writing had always been easy for me in my native language, and I enjoyed expressing myself through writing. However, I continued to struggle as a writer in English during my graduate study, facing each assignment as if I had rocks in my head and stomach. After many years of struggle and practice, I finally gained my current ease in English writing. I realized that writing not only helped me improve my English language proficiency but, more important, pushed me to think deeply, analytically, and logically. Writing about what I read helped me read with a critical lens and join the conversation in the literacy circle of my peers. Through my diligence in practicing this kind of writing, reading, and speaking, I grew academically.

When I started my work with English language learners (ELLs) in the New York City schools, I identified and empathized with students I saw struggling to write in English. Based on my own history as a struggling writer of English, I knew they should not wait in their learning to write until they gained full proficiency in speaking and reading English—especially since they were still in the process of developing their writing skills in their native language. As Kathleen Yancey states in her presidential address (2009), "We expect complex thinking to develop *alongside* and *with* beginning skills . . . because perhaps as never before, learning to write is a lifelong process" (331). ELLs needed to learn to write for their academic pursuit as well as for their language learning. But how to help ELLs develop their writing skills while they were learning English was a puzzle to all of us who were struggling to help them succeed in their studies. It was through my decade's work in schools populated with ELLs that I gradually learned—by observing in classrooms, examining writing samples, and listening to teachers and students talk about their teaching and learning experiences—how ELLs developed as writers in English.

My work today helping ELLs develop as writers in English deals with some regrets and wishes I held deep inside myself: I regret I had to wait until I was in graduate school to first learn how to write in English. I wish that I had taught my students to write during my seven years of teaching English. I often think of those students and hope my teaching didn't do too much damage to them in their academic pursuit. These regrets and wishes have always served as both motivation and inspiration for my current work with ELLs. I hope my work defining ELLs' writing development will contribute to an understanding of ELLs' transition to becoming English writers and to the improvement of writing instruction for all ELLs.

This book presents a discussion of the writing development that English language learners at the upper elementary and secondary levels are making as they proceed from their native language to English and provides suggestions for teaching this process. Over the past two decades, the number of

English language learners in the United States has grown from twenty-three million to forty-seven million, or by 103 percent. By 2030, immigrant children should account for 40 percent of the school-age population (U.S. Census Bureau 2003). Because educational advancement in the United States is closely tied to English proficiency, students from linguistically and culturally diverse backgrounds are approximately three times more likely to be low achievers than high achievers, and two times more likely to drop out than their native-English-speaking peers (Urban Institute 2005).

Research indicates that new immigrant students in grades 6 through 12 encounter the most challenges in schools due, in part, to their age when they enter the United States, a critical age in their lives; the high academic demands placed on them; and the limited time before graduation. Among these preteen or teenage newcomers, a majority are fluent speakers in their native language and are able to read and write in their first language, though some may not be performing at grade level (Genesse et al. 2005). When they enter the schools in the United States, they have to make many transitions—linguistically, culturally, socially, and academically. Among all the academic tasks ELLs face, learning to write in English probably presents the greatest challenge. Yet writing is often taught merely as a language exercise to ELLs. As my work illustrates, any progress newly arrived ELLs in upper elementary and secondary levels can make in learning to write in English directly relates to the linguistic and academic demands they face and to their social and cultural adjustment to their new world.

This book is, first, for all teachers—ESL, regular classroom, or content-area—who teach at the upper elementary and secondary levels and who have ELLs in their classrooms, particularly, recently arrived ELLs. Teaching writing to such students is especially difficult at the secondary level, where content-area subjects, taught in academic English, are the main curriculum.

Most literacy instruction for ELLs in the United States focuses on grammar skills, vocabulary building, content reading, or speaking and listening. Little attention is paid to writing development, and a focus on writing as a tool for thinking and communicating at the beginning and even at the intermediate level is a rarity (Harklau and Pinnow 2009). The emphasis on the surface structure of English may enable ELLs to achieve enough English proficiency to compose proper English sentences in correctly formatted monolingual papers, but it does not support them as competent writers and thinkers.

Much research (Calkins 1994; Hillocks 1995; Graves 1983) indicates that writing deepens thinking, expands reading comprehension, and reinforces language skills. Recently, literacy instruction for ELLs has included more writing, but as Samway (2006) reported in her research on writing instruction for ELLs: there is "lots of writing, but not much authentic writing" (158). Writing is a multidimensional process. It involves word-level skills, cognitive abilities, and higher-order thinking. Developing and orchestrating the various writing skills presents many challenges, even to first-language learners (Snelling and Van Gelderen 2004). Due to added linguistic demands, ELLs need more time and more instruction than first-language learners to develop the writing skills and abilities—through frequent, authentic writing opportunities and systematic scaffolding of their writing development. This book helps teachers to understand how ELLs make transitions from writing in their native language to writing in English, and then provides them with specific strategies to scaffold ELLs' writing development.

My discussion of ELLs' writing development challenges the view commonly held by many applied linguists that ELLs have to develop a certain degree of oral language proficiency before they learn to write for authentic purpose (Davis, Carlistle, and Beeman 1999; Dufva and Voeten 1999; Lanauze and Snow 1989; Lumme and Lehto 2002). This book addresses the questions frequently raised by teachers: How can we teach the ELLs to write when they don't have a command of basic English skills? How can we help ELLs make the transition from writing in their native language to writing in English? My responses to these questions draw from my extensive work with teachers in New York City schools as we searched for ways to improve instruction for ELLs and promote authentic reading and writing in literacy instruction for all students.

This book also contributes to the research on second-language writing. Research on ELL writing in grades K through 12 is very limited. In the most updated review of research on second-language writing, Harklau and Pinnow (2009) state:

> Second-language writing is a relatively new field drawing from second-language acquisition and composition studies. Most of the work to date has focused on the college level, and research specifically addressing adolescent second- and foreign language writing remains sparse, characterized by isolated studies with few sustained threads of inquiry. (126)

My work is more of a practitioner-oriented guide than a well-designed empirical study. I join authors like Freeman and Freeman (1996, 2002, 2005), Samway (2006), Peregoy and Boyle (2005), and Gibbons (2002), whose work on teaching and learning of K–12 ELLs came from their close association with classroom teachers and is known as teacher friendly but woven with research and practice. All these authors stress the importance of learning relevancy, authentic communication, respect for students' language and cultural backgrounds, and systematic scaffolding of ELLs' language development through meaningful reading and writing in content areas.

Though grounded in the same philosophic principles, my work differs from their work. While their research studies young ELLs who are becoming writers, mine examines older ELLs who are becoming writers of English. In other words, the ELLs discussed in my work, rather than emerging as writers, are already writers in their first language and are learning to become proficient writers of English. The process of their transition from being writers of their native language to writers of English is much more complicated than young bilingual children's quest to become emergent writers. The writing development of young bilingual children is similar to that of young monolingual English-speaking children: from scribble or drawings, to invented spelling writing, to conventional writing.

Most ELLs who came to the United States in upper elementary or secondary grades are able to read and write in their native language and have already gone through this emerging period in their native-language learning (Genesse et al. 2005). What they need while learning English is to make the transition from their first-language writing to English and from writing personal narrative to more formal academic writing. My discussion highlights the role ELLs' native language plays in their becoming writers of English. Research of contrastive rhetoric (Raimes 1991; Leki 1991) suggests that ELLs' writing backgrounds are an important resource rather than a hindrance in learning to write English. Connor (1996) pointed out that ELL writers "bring to the classroom ways of structuring discourse, interacting with audiences, and valuing knowledge that they have learned in their first language, employing some of these social practices as they write in English" (26). Cummins (1979) and Garcia (2002) emphasized the transfer of L1 (first language) literacy knowledge in ELLs' learning to write in L2 (second language). All these studies on second-language writers address the importance of background and native language, but few have shown how ELL learners make the transition from writing in their native language to writing in English. This book fills this gap and may provoke further discussion on this topic.

My Decade's Work in New York City Schools

In the course of my extensive work in schools over the past ten years, I have gathered the work of ELL writers and developed a model of how ELLs make the transition to fluency as they learn to write in English. From 1997 to 2007, I worked two to three days a month in New York City schools. There were three phases to my work in the city.

The first phase, which lasted five years, started in Chinatown at Dr. Sun Yat Sen Middle School. The majority of the student population in this school were Chinese-speaking immigrants; 34.5 percent were recently arrived newcomers, who were all on free lunch. During those five years, I worked closely with school administrators, staff, and all ESL and bilingual teachers to transform the school from a lower-performing school to being in the top 10 percent (twenty-fourth out of 220) of middle schools in New York City. The school became a learning community where the administrators joined regular faculty study groups during lunchtime or before or after school. The literacy coaches were selected from among the faculty, and their classrooms became teaching-demonstration sites for the school. The teachers in the building conducted workshops on professional development (PD) days, and visited each other's rooms regularly for instructional improvement and to assess the students in different learning settings. My five years in this school were documented in my book *An Island of English: Teaching ESL in Chinatown* (2003). During those years, I was able to work closely with teachers and students in classrooms, tracking students' progress and debriefing about lessons. As a writing specialist, I had a keen interest in how students grow as writers. I learned about teaching writing to ELLs while working in those classrooms by observing students in their classrooms and by examining their work at various stages of their growth as language learners, readers, and writers.

Later, my work expanded to several other Chinatown middle as well as elementary schools, where I continued to work with ESL specialists, regular classroom teachers, and ELL students in their rooms. That was the second phase, and lasted two years. Due to the limited time and increased number of schools involved, I was unable to spend as much time working with teachers in their classrooms or tracking students' progress consistently as I had previously, since I had to hop from one classroom to another and visit different schools on different days. Working in both middle and elementary schools during those two years, I began to see a general pattern of bilingual/ELL young children emerging as writers and to notice the differences between young children and older children in their transition to becoming English speakers and writers. Because I could speak Mandarin (Standard Chinese), the schools also asked me to meet regularly with the parents of the immigrant students. Working with these parents gave me an understanding of the ELLs' home literacy, family background, and living experiences. Whenever parents learned that a Mandarin-speaking educator would meet with them, they would try hard to attend the meeting. Some changed their work schedule, some traveled across the city to get to the schools, and some asked their friends or relatives to tape my talk if they were not able to attend the meetings. I will never forget one parent's words and her straight look into my eyes when she asked me at a workshop, "How would you help me to help my child to be able to stand there like you as a professional, speaking to a crowd?" I don't remember exactly if I fumbled in answering such an unexpected question, but I did feel a heavy weight on my shoulders as an educator at that moment.

After two years of working in the Chinatown schools, I was hired to lead the ELL Literacy Initiative in Region 9 to give special support to ESL and bilingual teachers. That was the third phase, the last three years of my work in the city schools. Throughout this project, I worked with ESL and bilingual teachers in fourteen schools from lower Manhattan to the Bronx, including Chinatown and Spanish Harlem—all heavily populated with immigrant students. During this phase, I made three-day monthly visits, working one day with an elementary school group, one day with a middle school group, and one day with a high school group. Each group consisted of classroom teachers, ESL specialists, and assistant principals from four to five schools. These educators would take one day a month away from their teaching or routine work to join our study group. On our monthly study day, we discussed our assigned reading, designed lesson plans, visited each other's teaching, and debriefed our classroom visits as a whole group. In between the monthly study days, Karen Low, the regional ESL specialist and a former middle school principal, followed up with weekly visits to the participant-teachers in their classrooms. In these visits, she helped the teachers implement the lessons we had discussed during the study day and solve specific problems in their teaching.

During our three-year project, we worked hard to implement language instruction to ELLs through authentic reading and writing. We introduced developmentally appropriate, culturally relevant, quality literature to the classrooms along with daily writing for communication and accountable talk. Together as a group, we created ways to assess students' progress individually as readers, writers, and language learners. We also sought ways to ensure time for real teaching and learning while dealing with high-stakes test demands.

It was during this decade in New York City schools that I determined that there are roughly four types of ELLs: (1) those who have strong first-language literacy; (2) those who lack first-language literacy or who had an interrupted formal education; (3) those who are long-term ELLs (over six years); and (4) those who are mainstreamed in regular classrooms after passing the required English language tests.

The first group of ELLs usually quickly becomes the fourth group, mainstreamed into regular classrooms after being in the ESL program for two or three years. Once they are mainstreamed, they are still very much ELLs but have to learn the same curriculum as their English-proficient peers, with little extra support. The second group is a challenging one;

usually the students of this group become long-term ELLs (the third group). Some have spent their entire school career, from elementary to high school, as ELLs. These long-term ELLs may have proficiency in oral English communication but have problems with academic reading and writing. Many eventually drop out of school.

Teaching ELLs is challenging, especially at the secondary level, where the curriculum is demanding, grade standards are stressed, and teaching is departmentalized. In addition, ELLs are placed in grades according to their age no matter what background of education they have, and they are expected to graduate at the same time as their English-proficient peers. With the No Child Left Behind Act imposed on U.S. schools, both teachers and ELLs are facing unrealistic teaching and learning expectations.

In U.S. public schools, ELLs are provided with different services depending on school budget, resource availability, and state policies. These services include self-contained ESL programs (content based), bilingual programs, and pull-out and push-in ESL programs. Research suggests (Carrasquillo and Rodriguez 1995) that self-contained ESL programs in content-subject study offer the best way to develop language skills and subject-content knowledge in ELLs. Usually ELLs are provided with two to three years of service in these programs. If they need more, they are considered long-term ELLs. However, due to budget cuts and a shortage of resources, most schools in New York City cannot afford self-contained ESL or bilingual programs. Also, in many schools, the number of students (at least twenty needed to make a class due to budget limits) can't make a self-contained class at each grade level. Therefore, pull-out (taking ELLs for ESL service) and push-in (ESL teacher coming in the classroom for service) ESL programs are the most common practices in our schools. With only one or two periods a day in this kind of ESL program, ELLs spend most of day in the regular classrooms studying the same curriculum along with their English-proficient peers.

As a writing specialist, I had a particular interest in ELLs' writing development while working to help them develop their overall English literacy. Unfortunately, writing instruction for ELLs was often presented as language exercises in which students practiced grammar skills or vocabulary usage, similar to monolingual students' making sentences with spelling words or writing sentences to practice capitalization or punctuation. During my first year of work in Dr. Sun Yat Sen Middle School, we began to promote language learning for ELLs through meaningful speaking, reading, and writing. This was a tremendous challenge for the teachers of ELLs, especially at the beginning level. It appeared to be impossible to engage them with meaningful speaking, reading, and writing before they had developed a certain level of oral English language proficiency.

Together, their teachers and I searched for ways to discover the students' potential. We tried different strategies, made many errors, and let students teach us how to teach them. Every year we made some progress. By the end of my third year in this middle school, quality literature reading and meaningful writing across the curriculum were adopted in almost every classroom for beginning ELLs. My first five years' work was solely in this Chinatown middle school, and I continued to work with the teachers from this school later, when my work was expanded to over a dozen other schools. I examined thousands of pieces of student writing; many were collected by teachers to examine their teaching techniques and track their students' progress and many were brought to our monthly meetings for discussion. When I had any chance to work with the teachers in their classrooms, I would read through the students' work from notebooks, writing logs, and portfolios to understand how they were learning to be English writers, readers, and language learners and to figure out what would be the next step for them. When I worked at Dr. Sun Yat Sen Middle School, I had the most access to the students' work as well as opportunities to interview students and teachers, which enabled me to make sense of the students' writing and see their progress in context. That access was like a treasure island to me.

In the past decade, I repeatedly examined all the students' writing I collected, trying to make sense of the ELLs' learning process and to connect their work with the strategies the teachers used in their instruction. After examining these thousands of pieces of writing produced by beginning ELLs at upper elementary to secondary grades, I found a general pattern of ELL writing development from their first language to English. Most ELLs in the school worked hard and were eager to become readers and writers in English. They knew that their ability to make it in this new world depended on the development of their English language skills. I concur with many bilingual researchers that long-term bilingual and dual-language programs are more effective for literacy achievement for ELLs, and that we should value the students' home languages equally as much as English, society's dominant language in our schools. However, in our current educational system and political era, this belief remains an ideal rather than a reality. Of the bilingual programs I encountered in the New York City school system, the majority are transitional programs, where students are given service for two to three years and then must exit to mainstream classrooms to study along with their English-proficient peers. In these schools, teachers constantly face the challenge of helping their ELLs make effective transitions from their learning in the first language to developing both communicative and academic English proficiency in two or three years (under the NCLB Act, ELLs have to take the identical standardized test as their English proficiency peers after one year of being in U.S. schools).

In my discussion of ELLs' writing development, I use writing samples mostly from Chinese ELLs to illustrate my points because most of the writing samples that came to me were written by ELLs in Chinatown schools. However, I include some samples from Spanish-speaking students to show how the development patterns are similar among ELLs with different linguistic backgrounds. In my decade's work in the New York City schools, I spent the most time in Chinatown schools heavily populated with Chinese-speaking ELLs. It took years of consistent work to develop a program that could show teachers how to help ELLs grow as writers of English by implementing daily writing into every classroom. The ELLs in most of the Chinatown schools where I worked were given opportunities to write daily in all classes—ESL/bilingual, regular, and content area. The ELLs there were allowed to compose in their first language and switch between languages to express themselves. I gathered volumes of writing from ELLs, mostly the Chinese-speaking ones: journal writing, personal narratives, essays, science reports, poems, and fiction stories in different forms, for different purposes, and in different classes.

learning. Many applied linguists believe that ELLs have to develop a certain level of oral language proficiency before they can express their ideas in written English (Davis, Carlistle, and Beeman 1999; Dufva and Voeten 1999; Lanauze and Snow 1989; Lumme and Lehto 2002). Meaningful writing is rarely taught to or required for newly arrived ELLs. Instead, they are given language-skill exercises to practice spelling, grammar rules, and sentence patterns. Writing for self-expression or learning discussion has to wait until they reach a certain degree of oral English proficiency. Later, when they are required to write, they tend to focus on correct English rather than on the expression of thoughts, a writing habit formed while studying the language. One of the dilemmas older ELLs may face is that their English proficiency doesn't match the thoughts they yearn to convey through writing. As one ELL writer expressed: "I had to copy the sentences from the book, here one and there one, to make my writing. Or I don't know how to write in English." This is a common practice among ELLs struggling to write.

Many nonnative writers of English who came to an English-speaking country after middle school claim that they were never taught to write in English. Writing was not part of language learning. A friend of mine described his development as a writer in English, which is common for non-English-speaking writers:

> I studied English formally for eight years from middle school to college in my country, but was never taught how to write or barely wrote anything meaningful in English while learning English. I learned grammar and vocabulary, and learned to read. When I came to study in the US, I had to write papers in English. I wrote, wrote and wrote endless papers. Very bad at first. When I got my papers back, they were full of corrections by the professors, who couldn't follow what I tried to say. After many years of struggling, finally I could write decent papers, though it's still not easy for me. I was a good writer in my native language. That is good and also bad in my development as a writer in English. The good part is: I love to write, and I have the desire to learn to write well in English and I know how to organize my writing. The bad part is: I got frustrated easily, as I know how well I could express myself in my native language, but I couldn't do so in English. That made me so frustrated sometimes. To develop as a writer in English is like fumbling through a tunnel blindly without directions.

How can we help our ELLs reduce their frustration as they learn to write in English? Must they wait until they develop a certain oral and reading proficiency before they begin to write for self-expression? Research in L2 acquisition (Cummins 1981; Thomas and Collier 1997) indicates that it takes two to three years for ELLs to develop communicative language proficiency, and five to seven or more years to develop academic language proficiency. ELLs, like their English-proficient peers, need to learn new knowledge and develop their academic skills while acquiring a new language. They can't afford to wait two or three years before they begin to engage in meaningful writing activities.

Research in second-language acquisition and bilingual/biliteracy in past decades confirms that literacy transfers across languages (Cummins 1979, 1981; Edelsky 1982; Morage e Silva 1988). Writers who are good in their native language tend to have a better understanding of the writing process and a better concept than weak writers of certain techniques, such as a sense of audience, a sense of organization, and a tendency to use details to support their thesis or elaborate their ideas. Among the hundreds of ELLs at all levels I interviewed over the past two decades, those who were good writers in their native language learned to write in English more rapidly and with less frustration, and many of them eventually enjoyed writing in English. But those who didn't like to write in their native language experienced tremendous difficulty in learning to write in English, and tended to avoid writing as much as possible, especially in a second language. Teaching ELLs to write includes helping them learn to enjoy writing and apply the writing skills they learned in their first language to their second-language writing.

Based on the literacy transfer theory, which holds that ELLs transfer their literacy skills in L1 to their learning in L2 such as linguistic knowledge and sense of audience, I proposed to all the schools where I worked that beginning ELLs be allowed to write in their first language—not only in ESL and bilingual classrooms, but also in every subject area—before they were able to express themselves fully in English. This enabled ELLs to engage in meaningful writing from day one when they came to our school. Their constant writing deepened their learning in all subject areas and made their language learning more meaningful and personally relevant (Fu 2003).

The Four Stages of ELLs' Writing Development

By examining the writing samples of beginning ELLs, I uncovered a general pattern in ELLs' transitions to English-writing fluency. These transitions can be divided into four stages: Stage 1, first language; Stage 2, code-switching or mixed language; Stage 3, inter-language (English writing in the native-language syntax); and Stage 4, close to Standard English. These stages are represented by the four writing samples in Figures 2.1, 2.2, 2.3, and 2.4, produced by a fourth-grade Chinese-speaking ELL, Xuhua, during his first year of schooling in the United States.

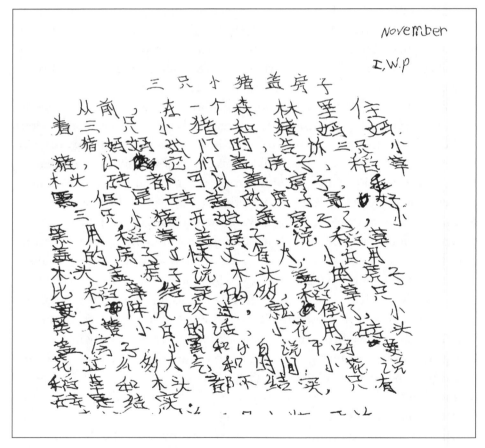

Figure 2.1   *Xuhua's Chinese Writing*

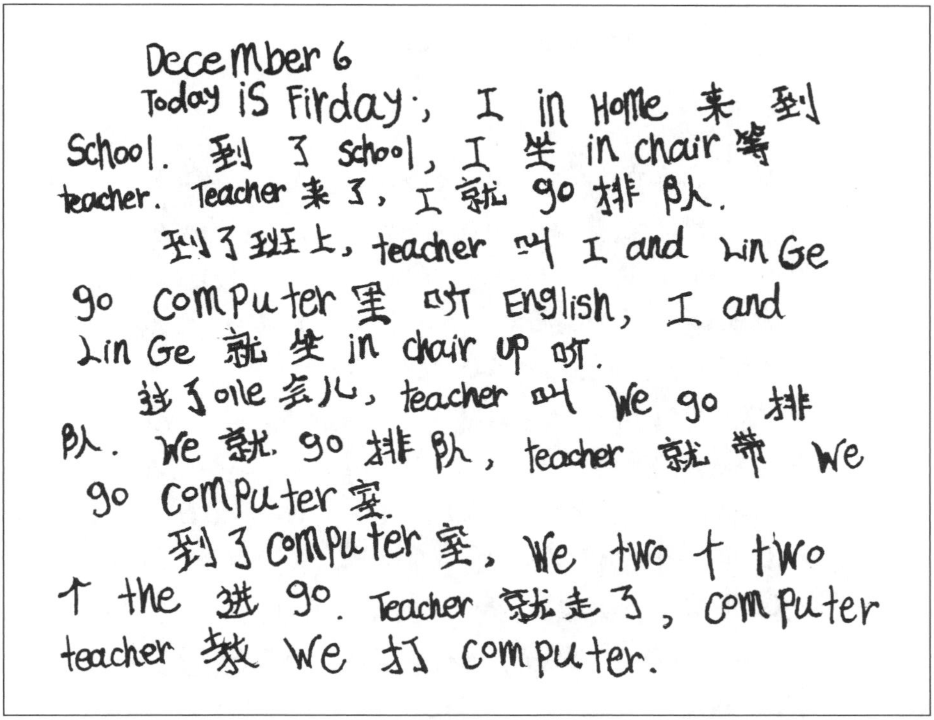
December 6
Today is Firday; I in Home 来到
School. 到了 school, I 坐 in chair 等
teacher. Teacher 来了, I 就 go 排队.
到了班上, teacher 叫 I and Lin Ge
go computer 室 听 English, I and
Lin Ge 就 坐 in chair up 听.
过了one 会儿, teacher 叫 We go 排
队. We 就 go 排队, teacher 就 带 We
go computer 室.
到了computer 室, We two 个 two
个 the 进 go. Teacher 就走了, computer
teacher 教 We 打 computer.

Figure 2.2 *Xuhua's Mixed-Language Writing*

During his first year of study in the United States, Xuhua was placed in a regular fourth-grade classroom and pulled out two periods a day for ESL service. He participated in daily writing workshop in his regular classroom and continued to work on his writing in the ESL room. Before he could express himself in English, he wrote in his native language, Chinese, and gradually he transitioned from writing in mixed languages to English writing. The freedom of choice to compose in any language or any form, such as native language or mixed language, that he was given enabled him to engage in meaningful writing throughout his first year in the American school. Xuhua's writing samples demonstrate a steady development from his native language to English in the four transitional stages. However, we don't see this orderly development for all students in a class from month to month, due to the differences in their first-language writing ability, their

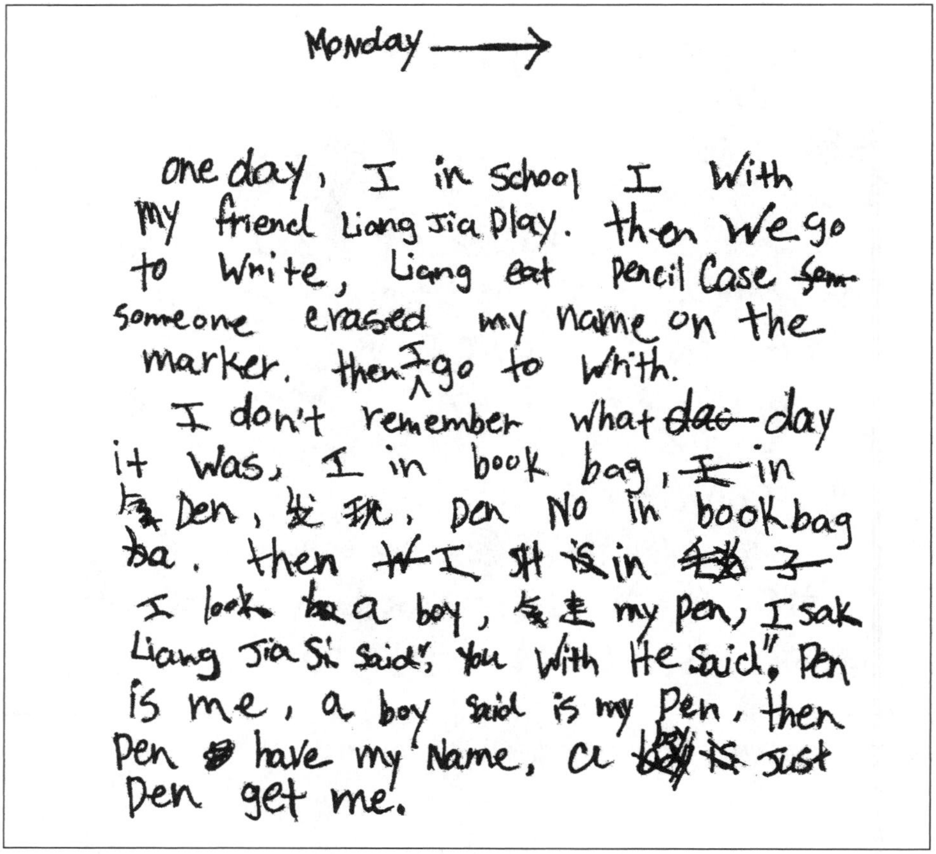

Monday →

one day, I in School I With my friend Liang Jia Play. then We go to Write, Liang eat pencil Case ~~Som~~ someone erased my name on the marker. then I go to Writh.

I don't remember what ~~dae~~ day it Was, I in book bag, ~~I~~ in 写 pen, 发现, pen No in bookbag ba. then I 开 in I look a boy, 拿走 my pen, I sak Liang Jia Si said", You With He said", pen is me, a boy said is my pen, then pen have my Name, a 就 Just pen get me.

Figure 2.3 *Xuhua's Inter-Language Writing*

English proficiency, their learning habits and styles, and the length of time they have been in American schools. Because of these differences, we see all four transitional stages in ELLs' writing occurring simultaneously in one class throughout the school year.

The four stages of ELLs' writing development described here are different from the Five Levels of Language Proficiency defined by TESOL (Teachers of English to Speakers of Other Languages) Standards (2006). The definition of the five levels of language proficiency of TESOL

Book Review

I have the book. This it the place for me, by Joanna Cole, it was funny story. Why it was a funny story because Morty the bear was always breaking things in his house, he was so big, he couldn't help it. He broke his chair, his table, his door and his anything, but he did not fix his anything. He found a new house, but it had a dragon, and it was too small, and it was too thine and it could sink sink, and it was scary. So he came back to his old house to fix the door, window, table and chair, now the old house was as good as new, and Morty say, "This is the place for me, it is much better than my old house, Morty was happy to came to his old house to fix anythings, and his house was new.

Figure 2.4 *Xuhua's Writing Approaching to Conventional English*

Standards focuses on language development (linguistic skills) from low-proficient to high-proficient levels as Chart 2.5 indicates.

My definition of the four stages of the ELLs' writing development also differs from the seven-stage model of L2 writing development in adolescents proposed by Valdes (1999). Sharing features of the TESOL Standards, Valdes' model also presents a transition from zero or lower to the higher levels indicated in Chart 2.6.

Level 1 Starting Up	Level 2 Beginning	Level 3 Developing	Level 4 Expanding	Level 5 Bridging Over
Words, phrases, or memorized chunks of language	Written language with phonological, syntactic, or semantic errors that often impede the meaning of the communication	Written language with phonological, syntactic, or semantic errors that may impede the communication but retain much of its meaning	Written language with minimal phonological, syntactical, or semantic errors that do not impede the overall meaning of the communication	Written language approaching comparability to that of English-proficient peers

Chart 2.5   *Productive Language: English Language Learners Produce in English*

Stage 1	Writes lists of familiar English words
Stage 2	Writes simple unconnected sentences
Stage 3	Can write very short connected discourse
Stage 4	Can write short connected discourse
Stage 5	Can write longer segments of connected discourse
Stage 6	Demonstrates little or no audience awareness
Stage 7	Sense of audience begins to develop

Chart 2.6   *Valdes' Model: Stages of L2 Writing Development in Adolescents*

Both TESOL's five levels of language development and Valdes' model of the seven stages of writing development start from the ELL student's English ability level, moving from very limited to high proficiency. Unlike these definitions of ELLs' learning development, the transition I suggest starts from what ELLs can do. I see their first literacy level as the starting point, thus validating their abilities as writers. The framework that embraces my idea is grounded in the "funds of knowledge" theory, as defined by Moll and his colleagues (1992) and Martinez-Roldan and Franquiz's proposition (2009) on bilingual writers and speakers:

> A bilingual person does not have two separate sets of linguistic resources. Instead of being a "double-monolingual" person, a bilingual person has special linguistic resources beyond what a monolingual person in either of the languages has. Becoming bilingual, then, requires the ability to employ language resources from two codes strategically and with great sensitivity to contextual factors. (327)

These researchers of bilingualism proposed to identify students' home culture and language as promising, rather than deficient, "funds of knowledge." Based on their framework, I view ELLs who can read and write in their native language as able writers. The first stage of their development as writers of English arises from the rich fund of knowledge they hold in their native language. Garcia (2001) posited that we should learn what students can do in their native language and provide opportunities to build on that expertise. Thus, the term *development,* used to illustrate their writing transition in my work, differs from its usual meaning of moving from a lower to a higher level or from less to more proficiency, because the ELLs' first-language writing ability is more advanced than their English writing ability, as indicated in Chart 2.7.

This chart shows that ELLs' first-language literacy (L1) may be at the sixth-grade level while their English proficiency (L2) may be only at the first-grade level. When we help these students develop as English writers, it doesn't mean simply moving them from a lower writing ability to a higher writing ability but, rather, helping them attain what they already can do as a native language writer in a second language. In the same sense, when I use the term *transition* to describe the four stages of ELL writing development,

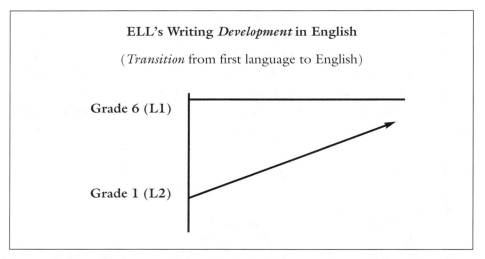

ELL's Writing *Development* in English

(*Transition* from first language to English)

Grade 6 (L1)

Grade 1 (L2)

Chart 2.7   *ELL's Writing Development in English*

it doesn't denote moving from one place to another. In other words, rather than using English to replace the ELLs' first language, students ideally will continue to develop their first-language writing skills while learning to write in English.

Helping ELLs develop as writers of English is similar to helping young children become writers. Chart 2.8 shows this parallel in writing development between ELLs and native-English language speakers.

I believe that to enhance writing development, we need to start from what students can do. We must not only legitimize any transition in their development but also provide support and guidance as they hone their writing skills at each transitional stage. In teaching emergent native-English speakers, we value their first, hardly discernible attempts at spoken language. We likewise must see ELLs' code-switching and inter-language writing as significant, natural stages in their learning to write in English; must recognize the important presence that their native language has in their lives; and must understand that "their location on the biliteracy continua may influence not only how students speak but also how they write" (Martinez-Roldan and Franquiz 2009, 327). It is common to find the presence of loan words, calques, and code-switching in ELLs' speech and writing.

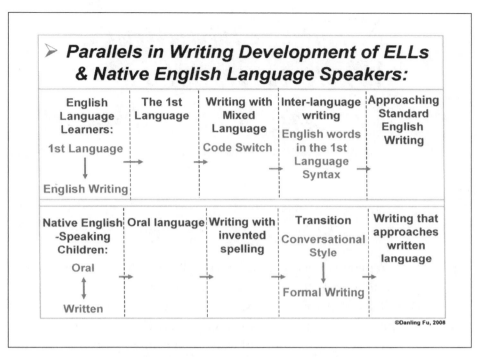

Chart 2.8   *Parallels in Writing Development of ELL's and Native English Language Speakers*

Of course, we need to recognize that differences exist in first-language literacy among ELLs. Some have strong first-language literacy; some have weak first-language literacy and are not at the grade level they should be; and some, with interrupted formal education, may not be able to read or write in their first language. For ELLs who can't read or write in their first language we can begin with their oral language or, like young children (three to five years old), help them learn to write as emergent writers. We need to tailor our instruction in scaffolding ELLs' writing development to fit where they are as literate individuals. The following chapters specifically address these issues. Chapters 3 and 4 focus on the important role that ELLs' native language plays in their development as writers of English and the transitions they make to gain fluency in English writing in general.

3 *Native-Language Writing in ELLs' Writing Development*

Many people believe that when ELLs write in English, they should completely bypass their native language. I, too, held this belief for many years and pushed myself to achieve this goal throughout my study as an English language learner, but never truly succeeded. Even today, with volumes of publications in English, I still sometimes think in Chinese, dream in Chinese, and mentally translate from Chinese to English, especially about the subjects I learned first in my native tongue such as medicine, mathematics, and science. After reflecting on my own journey in learning to write in English and examining other ELLs' writing development, I realized that ELLs' first-language writing plays an important role in their English writing development.

I was never taught how to write in English during my years of formal English study in China. I credit my progress as a writer in English today to my good writing skills in Chinese. I learned to write in Chinese and never stopped writing in Chinese while learning English. When I was later required to write essays in English during my graduate study, I used my native language to think, to plan, to organize, and to reason. My writing then involved a mental translation process from Chinese to English. And although my writing might often have sounded foreign to my English-speaking professors, with some awkward expressions or Chinese rhetoric, I could make myself understood and present my thoughts in an intellectually appropriate manner at the graduate level. I don't think I would have been able to produce such papers in English if I were a poor writer in my native language.

Years ago, I did a study on the writing processes that foreign students undergo on a college campus. Among the over two dozen international students I interviewed, all went through writing processes that were similar to mine. That study (Fu and Townsend 1998) indicates that students who are better writers in their native language learn to write in English with less frustration than students who are poorer writers in their native language. The former learn to write well eventually, while the latter try to avoid writing in English as much as they can.

Not long ago, I met a visiting scholar who was a science educator and a professor in a university in Taiwan. He told me that he had an ambitious plan to try to produce two papers during his one-year stay in the United States. I was quite puzzled by his "ambition," because producing two papers in a year without any teaching or other professional responsibility did not sound that ambitious to me. When I asked, "Why only two?" he told me, "I have to write them in English, which is very hard for me." I then asked, "Do you know what you want to write about?" After he replied with confidence, I suggested, "Why not write first in Chinese, and then translate it into English?" His response was "But I was told one should only think in English when writing in English." After I briefly presented my reasoning on this issue, he said he felt relieved and alive as a writer again. Later, I emailed him, asking how he was doing with his writing. His response, which was written in Chinese and which I translated, follows:

> When I could write first in Chinese, my writing flows. I can explain complicated concepts and ideas with precise language and depth of thinking. The writing is fluent and logical with solid substance. When I write in English, I can't reach the level as I want to, that is very frustrating. When I translate my work into English, I try hard not to translate words for words, that would sound too Chinese-English. In translation, I try to use English to express what I mean in my native language, so sometimes the English translation doesn't match my Chinese writing 100 percent. If I directly write in English, it usually takes three or four times longer than when I work the same topic in Chinese. Even so, the quality of my English writing is not as good as my Chinese writing.

A doctoral student of mine also shared with me a very interesting piece of data about a high school English writing class she observed in China. In that class, the English teacher asked her students to do some writing in English. Many students sat for a long time without producing anything. Finally, the teacher, out of the frustration, said to the students, "Just write in Chinese and then translate it into English later." The students immediately began writing. Figure 3.1 shows one student's writing and his translation.

The translation not only matches the Chinese writing quite accurately, but also demonstrates the writer's good command of English grammar

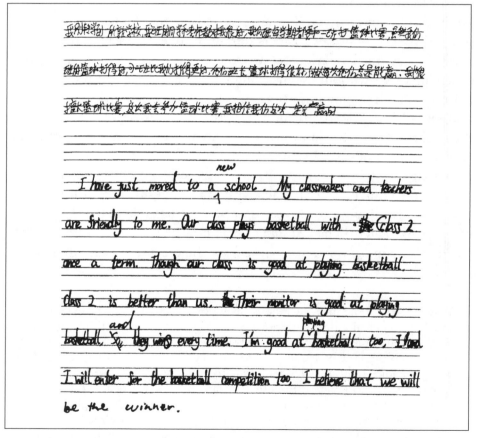

Figure 3.1   *An Example of One Student's Writing and His Translation*

and spelling. Once this student was allowed to write first (or draft) in his native language, he had no problems in expressing himself. The whole process took less time (and effort) than when he was forced to write only in English.

Historically, translating in ESL writing is discouraged and inhibited (Liu 2004). Forcing ELLs to think in English has some merit in language-learning practice, especially when their English proficiency (what they can do) matches their thinking level (what they know). Thinking (or drafting) in English will help ELLs write in more idiomatic English than translating, which tends to be contaminated with their native expressions. However, for ELL writers at the beginning and even intermediate stages, this practice constrains thinking capacity, limits expression, and frustrates them tremendously in their writing process.[1]

Once I gave a writing assignment to a group of teachers in a weekly workshop. I asked them to write something in any foreign language they had learned. They could choose their own topics, use the dictionary, and use translation or mixed-language methods if they needed to. Even if they knew no other language, they were encouraged to try to write using the dictionary and mixed language. The following day, everyone produced some writing and shared their work and process. One teacher explained that she had learned Spanish over thirty years ago but barely remembered any Spanish words. So she wrote first in English and then translated her writing into Spanish with the help of a dictionary. She was very proud of her piece, which follows:

> Pasado semana, yo took digital storytelling. Nosotras sat en cojin sillas en lugar con aire acondicionado. Ahora, yo dar ESL escritura. Nosotras tenuous duro sillas. Le luger ne tenuous pas aire acondicinado. Le tempa es La liente et Humedo. UNH necesidad puia comprar nuero suavo sillas atencion carecer de aire acondicionado as much.

---

[1] Cumming (1989) found in his study that L1 plays a positive role in L2 composing and that ESL writers use their L1 not just to retrieve and generate content but also to verify word choice and assess unfamiliar knowledge. Based on Cumming's research findings, if we allow students to use their native language to draft (think), we reduce 50 percent of the cognitive demand in their L2 composing.

When they come home, we will act like what we would do in China. We would prepare a big delicious meal for the family, . . . My parents got home at nearly midnight. We had our New Year's Eve dinner together. We talked, laughed, and enjoyed our time together till 2:00 in the morning. Though the food was not as delicious or didn't have the variety as we would have in China, we had a good time, and that still was the most significant time of the year for us.

Chinese New Year's celebration in China and in America is indeed very different, but in my heart, it is the same. It is always the beginning of the year, and on that day, I will always set the new goals and new resolutions for the New Year. On each New Year's Day, I want to walk into the New Year as a new person.

This piece paints a vivid picture of a new person emerging through his words and thinking. I was impressed with the maturity revealed in this piece. I shared this piece with other monolingual, English-speaking teachers. They were surprised, because this student had shown limited literacy skills in his English writing. The teachers appreciated that I was able to read these students' Chinese writing and gain much insight into their thoughts and feelings. From their writing, I learned that these children all had vivid memories of their lives in China. Their families have to endure much hardship in their new lives here, but one can see in this example the quiet determination, the strong unity of the family, and the beautiful love among the family members.

Building Content Knowledge Through Learning and Writing in the First Language

Most ELLs are struggling to learn the same content knowledge as their English-speaking peers with their limited language ability. In order to keep pace with their learning in the subject areas, bilingual programs provide content knowledge instruction in their native language. Learning in their first language enables ELLs to obtain new knowledge in different subject areas and to develop cognitively which, in turn, gives them the opportunity to develop their writing skills. The bilingual program at Dr. Sun Yat

Sen Middle School in New York's Chinatown is integrated with the social studies curriculum, where the ELLs study American history, government, and current events. By being actively engaged in reading, writing, and talking about historical and current events in their native language in the program, the ELLs were preparing not only for their education in America, but also for their present and future lives in this democratic world (Fu 2003). Had the students not been allowed to use their first language to study the content knowledge, they would not have been able to read, write, and talk about sophisticated topics, which would seriously delay their academic growth and leave them significantly behind their English-proficient peers.

In the bilingual social studies class, these students enjoyed comparing and contrasting their learning of America with their knowledge of China and their own experiences. For instance, while studying immigration in the 1920s, students were able to compare the experiences of those immigrants with their own. The following excerpt of a student's work, written in Chinese, about his people in Chinatown was produced while studying immigration in the United States.

> New York is like a land filled with gold, which magically attracts immigrants for centuries. Our Fuzhounese [people from Fuzhou City] are among those. . . . [M]ost of them were smuggled into this country. They risked their lives to come here, and paid a big fee to the smugglers. Their relatives loaned all the money . . . [they] needed for coming here. . . . [They] can't disappoint them and [they] have to work hard to pay them back. That is why some Fuzhounese have to do something illegal, because they need money badly. That is how our Fuzhounese got the bad reputation. But actually we Fuzhounese are the hardest workers. We are working hard to change the bad impression the people have on us. I am glad I am a Fuzhounese, because we are the hardest workers among all immigrants. I am determined to study hard and have a good future. I want to gain a good reputation for Fuzhounese and not let others continue to look down upon us Fuzhounese. I want every one to know we, Fuzhounese, are the strongest of all.

This student expressed strong feelings about being discriminated against in the Chinatown community where, as the most recent newcomers, his people were consigned to the bottom ranks of Chinatown society. His writing not only helps us understand his people, but also leads us to admire his loyalty to his people and determination to better his community.

Weekly, the ELLs wrote two to three pieces in their native language on the topics related to their content study. Even though the focus of the bilingual class was more on social studies content than on writing, regular writing opportunities in their native language deepened students' thinking on the topics they were studying, and enabled them to continue to improve themselves as writers. Among the students, first-language writing ability varied widely. Some were strong writers and some, whose first-language literacy was two or three years below grade level, struggled to write. The bilingual teacher had to teach social studies content while helping them continue to improve their reading and writing skills in their native language. Explaining how they helped their ELLs improve their writing, one teacher stated:

I have my students write two pieces each week, mostly essays. Many students never learned how to write essays in the Western styles in China, so I have to model how to write essays, like with an introduction and a conclusion. I showed them many examples and worked with the whole class for the first few weeks, then most students would eventually get it. About 20 percent would always have problems. They are probably at third or fourth grade level in their Chinese, and now they are in the eighth grade. Both the content and writing requirements are hard for those students. I spread those students in each group and pair them with strong students. I wish I could work with those struggling students individually more. But with 115 students, and with such a heavy content I have to cover, I hardly have any time to work with individuals. What I could do is to give those students more writing samples and use them as writing models. Sometimes, I confer with these students while others are working in groups. But I hate to take them out of group discussion because it is important for them to hear their peers. I also pair the struggling students with strong students. Before they turn in any work, they have to give it to their partners to proofread. I give those helpers some extra credits. With writing frequently in this way, the struggling students gradually develop their writing skills. Now they can write at least three paragraphs cohesively, while the others can write three pages. (quoted in Fu 2003, 78)

Based on the transfer theory of language learning (Cumming 1989), learning to write and frequent writing opportunities in their first language certainly help lay a strong literacy foundation for ELLs in their English writing and language development.

Working with ELLs Who Have Limited First-Language Literacy

Even though this book focuses on ELLs who have some first-language literacy (that is, who can read and write in their native language), it is important to address the issue of how to help the ELLs who have limited first-language literacy become writers. These ELL students are also called SIFE students, which stands for students with interrupted formal education. Ruiz-de-Velasco and Fix's (2000) study on immigrant students in U.S. secondary schools indicates that 20 percent of all ELLs at the high school level and 12 percent of ELLs at the middle school level have missed two or more years of schooling since age six. Their study points out that

> The single strongest predicator of academic success for newcomers, outside of English language fluency, is how much prior schooling students have had in their native countries. Students who learned basic grammar rules in their native language . . . are well positioned to make successful transition to English language literacy. (55)

We encountered the greatest challenge in educating the SIFE students in our schools. They had very diverse backgrounds, and their formal education had been interrupted for different reasons. I met one sixth-grade girl at Dr. Sun Yat Sen Middle School who didn't know how to write her name in Chinese. Later, I found out that she came from a family who had two children. Chinese government policy calls for "one child per family," so her family had to pay for her education. After this girl went to school for a year or two her family had to stop paying for her schooling, and she had to quit school until she came to America. In a Spanish Harlem middle school, I also met two boys from Mexican migrant worker families. They had been in the United States for four to five years, but they moved back and forth constantly between the United States and their home country, and rarely spent a complete year in one school setting. In my early study of four Laotian refugee teens, three couldn't read or write in their native language when they came to this country. The youngest was thirteen years old and had never attended school for a day before he came to the United States. During his first year in a U.S. school, he was shifted three times from one grade to another: from second grade to sixth grade and then back to the fourth grade because the school didn't know where to place him (Fu 1995). Ruiz-de-Velasco and Fix (2000) reported in their study that one teacher in California described that new refugee students in her middle school "did not know how to use a pencil and were unaccustomed to sitting in a classroom for extended periods or raising their hands to be recognized" (55). All these ELLs encountered tremendous difficulty in our schools.

Teaching these students to write proved immensely challenging. Their teachers and I tried various strategies, but found we had to treat each case differently, based on what the individual student could do first. For ELLs who couldn't even write their names in their native language, we guided their writing development as we did with young emergent writers: we let them draw first to express themselves, and then taught them the English words to label their pictures. We used English pattern books to help them learn to read sentence patterns, then they used the sentence patterns to write their own pattern books. We also encouraged ELLs with some limited first-language literacy to draw, and then let them label or write captions for their drawings in their native language. Zhao's writing sample is an example (see Figure 3.2).

Zhao, who was from a village in China, started sixth grade in a school in New York City, yet his native language literacy was probably at first-grade level. His ESL teacher started him with repetitive pattern books in reading and guided him to write by drawing and labeling. He labeled his drawings sometimes with Chinese words and sometimes with English words. Gradually he wrote captions for his drawings in Chinese mixed with English. By the end of the school year, he was more confident writing

Figure 3.2   *Zhao's Story-Drawing with the Caption in Native Language*

English pattern books (modeled after the pattern books he read) than writing in Chinese.

Mendoza came from Mexico. Three years earlier, he had come to join his parents in the United States. Since then he had moved with his parents to different states for jobs. He came to one of our middle schools in New York's Spanish Harlem in March, near the end of his sixth grade. When he came, he could write only a few words in Spanish and barely spoke any

English. We encouraged him to write as he spoke. At the beginning, he wrote a piece as he spoke his native language (see Figure 3.3); later his native writing was much more readable than his beginning work (see Figure 3.4).

Mendoza's later piece describes his impressions of New York City: it is big, has many buildings and has many cars passing by.

In working with SIFE ELLs, the key is to start where they are, no matter how old they are or in what grade they are placed in our schools. The native language may not be the starting point for students who have never learned to read or write. We need to guide them to write as we guide young emergent writers: to draw, to label, to write captions, or to write as they speak. Each student needs his/her own approach for success and the starting point for SIFE ELLs will be different from the ELLs who can read and write in their native languages.

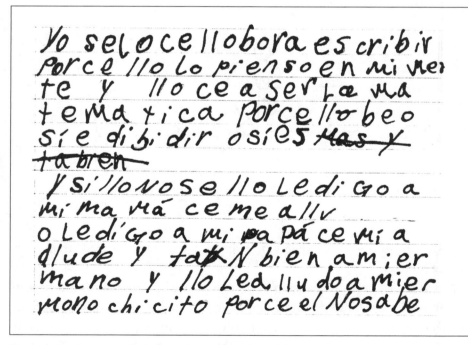

Figure 3.3 *Mendoza's Beginning Work in Spanish*

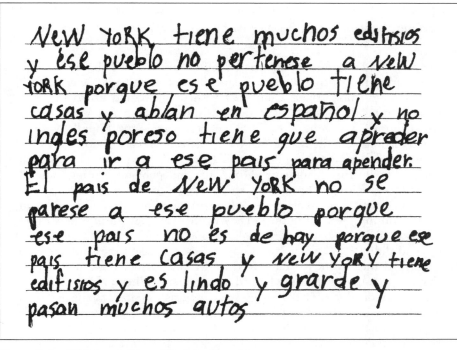

Figure 3.4 *Mendoza's Later Work in Spanish*

ELLs' Native-Language Writing in the ESL and Regular Classrooms

Most ESL and regular classroom teachers in the schools where I worked were unable to read or write their ELLs' native languages. This presented a dilemma when I first recommended that they let their ELLs write in their native tongue. Their question was "What is the point of letting them write in a language I can't understand?" That is a legitimate concern since we can't help our students improve their work when we can't understand what they write. In response, I nudged these teachers to adjust their traditional perspective and think for the benefit of the students. Once the teachers understood that letting the ELLs write in their first language is a way to help them grow as writers, they didn't feel odd about not being able to read the students' writing. One fifth-grade teacher in New York's PS 126 had two newly arrived ELLs in her class. Here she shares how she became to understand the value of letting her ELLs write in their native language:

> When Yi and Ping came to my class, I didn't know what I should do with them during the writing workshop time. They couldn't write any English and I couldn't understand Chinese. I wished they could go to the ESL teacher during this time, but it didn't always work that way. At first, I would use a few minutes to tutor them, teaching some English or do a shared reading with them and then leave them some seatwork on their own during the rest of the time. When you suggested that we should let them write in their native language during the independent writing time, I decided to give it try. Through the students who could speak Chinese, I let these two girls know that they could write anything they wanted to in Chinese during the writing time. They wrote every day during the writing time like their peers. At first, I was fascinated by their beautiful handwriting, and didn't know what it was about. Then, I asked the students who could read their work to translate their writing to me. I was amused by what they wrote. Their stories helped me understand them, not just as writers, but as individuals. They are two amazing girls who have so much to say. Now I really understand why we need to let our ELLs write in their native language, as their writing helps us to understand them and learn about them and their lives, this would help me know how to teach them better. Now I would write down their stories in English when I have a student retell their stories to me, and then I would let them read what I learned about their stories in English. This way I can use their writing to teach them English language skills by teaching them to read their own writing (rewritten in English).

Being allowed to write in their native language during the writing workshop time, Ping and Yi were able to engage in all kinds of meaningful writing along with their peers—personal narrative about their lives back in China and their family members, poems, and reading responses. Here is a poem written in Chinese by Ping:

My Mother's Eyes
Mom has a pair of juicy eyes,
They can make one feel joyful,
They can make me confess,
They can teach me lessons,
They can push me to work hard,

They can make me proud of myself,
They can stop me crying,
They can give me comfort.
I live in my mother's eyes every day,
I feel warm and happy.
Oh, my mother's eyes are great and magic.

Ping was a quiet student who arrived in this country at the beginning of fifth grade. She didn't speak any English. Every day she spent two hours in the ESL room and the rest of the school day in the regular fifth-grade classroom. At the beginning of the school year, she was learning basic skills in the ESL room: simple sentence patterns and pedestrian vocabulary. When she was in the regular class, as she described, "I couldn't understand anything, and just sat there watching the teacher and other students. It was boring, and I wished I could stay in the ESL room all the time." Once the teachers let her write in Chinese, she wrote every day. She wrote in the regular classroom and continued her writing in the ESL room. She wrote throughout her first year at PS 126. The following is an excerpt, written in Chinese, of a reading response to a Chinese book she read:

Feeling of Separation

I read a book recently, and its title is *A Cat in the Rain*. There are four short stories in this book, and one of them touched me the most, its title is Feeling of Separation. This story is about how a girl felt about separation, or how separation makes her feel like. Here is the story: once there was a girl, who had no brothers or sisters. She was lonely. She wanted to have a dog. One day, she found a street dog. She took him home. They loved each other. But a few days later, the dog got lost in the woods. The girl went everywhere looking for the dog, and found him nowhere. Later, she found another small dog. She took him home. Soon, she was inseparable from this little dog. But a few days later, this little dog died. She was terribly sad. Why did her dog either get lost or die? She cried for a long time. From this experience, she learned about separation: Separation is a feeling of loss or a memory, but it shouldn't always be sadness. She decided to cherish the sweet memories with her dogs and but not live in sadness so that she could continue to enjoy her dogs in her memory throughout her life.

I was very touched by this story, because I used to have a little dog myself, her name was Dongdong. She was very sweet. We spent over a year together, and loved each other. But when we left China, we had to give her to others. I miss her and many other relatives left behind in China, especially my grandma. My grandma loved me and always helped us whenever we were in need. Now I am far away from her, and other friends. I was very sad. Reading this story, I identified the feeling of separation. . . .

Ping wrote every day and shared her writing with Yi, mostly during the peer-sharing time, because Yi was the only one who could fully understand her writing. Yi and Ping became inseparable friends. While continuing to write in Chinese, Ping also experimented with writing in English. In January, four months after studying in the school, Ping started to produce English writing, with the most intimate topics in her life: her dog, her grandma, and her mother. In January, she wrote her dog story in English:

My dog
In my China home, I have a dog. My dog is very lovely. I like my dog. My dog is little. Its fur is yellow. My dog runs very fast. Its eyes a red, big and circular. He is very beautiful. Its ears are very lovely. My dog's nose is black. My dog likes to eat meat and drink mild. I like to play with my dog. My dog is lovely and beautiful, I like my dog!

Compared to her writing in Chinese, Ping's dog story written in English is much more basic, and doesn't reveal her true competence as a writer and a thinker. This piece is limited by her English vocabulary and English skills. To her, it was a big step, from only writing in Chinese to composing in English. Because she continued to write in her native language while learning to develop English skills, she was able to fully express herself, and she continued to soar as a writer and a thinker.

Assessing Native Language Writers When Teachers Can't Understand Their Work

It certainly sounds impossible to assess ELLs' native-language writing or work with them when we can't read their work. However, as parents, we often encourage our children to do some math, science, or computer work that is beyond our understanding. It simply makes us feel good to see our children work diligently on the subjects we know are important for their academic pursuit, even though we may not understand what they do. As teachers, we should hold this same attitude toward our ELLs when we let them write in their native language in our class. First, we should think that they are not writing for us. They are writing for their own benefit as writers and thinkers and for their literacy practice.

I asked a dozen teachers who were unable to read and write in Chinese how they assessed their ELLs' writing in Chinese. A common response from them was: "As long as they write and produce some writing, I give them credit. I assess their effort rather than content, since the length of their writing does tell me how much they were engaged in writing." Usually, the students were pretty serious about their writing even though they knew their teachers couldn't understand it. They preferred to write with their peers during writing workshop time, rather than being pulled out to do something else, such as reading simple books or doing language exercises with their teachers.

We should also let ELLs participate in other writing workshop activities such as peer conference, teacher conference, and author's chair. During the peer conference time, we should let them share their work with the students who can understand it. Sharing their work with their peers makes them feel like writers. Ping's teacher let Ping, Yi, and two other students who could speak their language form a peer-response group where they shared their work and listened to each other's comments. Ping and Yi usually listened quietly to the other two peers as they read their work, and the other two peers asked a lot of questions about Ping and Yi's writing, since they hadn't used their Chinese enough to fully understand Ping's and Yi's stories. The conversation in this group, which traveled between Chinese and English, benefited all the group members in terms of language learning and writing improvement.

The teacher in Ping and Yi's class worked out creative strategies to involve her ELLs with teacher conference and author's chair sharing. She illustrated her practice as follows:

I try to see my ELLs as regularly as I would do my other students, but my conference with them would be different from that with my other students. At first, I relied on the students who could speak their language help me with the conference, letting them translate their work to me, or tell me what their writing was about. Or sometimes, I would have those students write down the main ideas of their writing for me and I would ask questions through them about their writing to the ELLs. The purpose of my conference at that point was not to help them improve their work, but rather to show my interest in their writing, my care for their writing and my desire to understand their writing. Later when my ELLs were able to communicate with me in some English, I would ask them to draw pictures to show me what they wrote about. And together, we would write captions in English for the pictures they drew. This turned out to be an English speaking and writing activity in the context of their writing, which became an interesting and meaningful language activity for the ELLs as well. Then during the author's chair, they share with the class their pictures with captions. That was really great for the ELLs and also for the whole class to hear their work.

The ESL teacher had more one-on-one time with the ELLs to turn their native language writing into picture-stories with English captions. Through working with the ELLs in this picture-writing activity, the teachers discovered what vocabulary and language skills the ELLs needed to learn in order to express themselves. For instance, in helping Ping use drawing to retell a story about her sister, the teachers could teach her the English words, phrases, and basic sentence structures she needed to express herself in words. Through turning this piece into her picture story with English captions, Ping learned the following words and phrases:

younger sister and older sister

being naughty and tell lies

play toys

eat meals and have snacks

yell at and cry out

hot temper

be patient

bite and eat

neighbors

climb the mountains

rest, sleep, and take a break

It is much more meaningful to build vocabulary and learn spelling and sentence structures based on what our students themselves need to express rather than teaching them skills we think they need.

My proposal of letting ELLs write in their native language to expand their first-language literacy while learning English may encounter challenges. A school administrator at one of my workshops stated, "In the NCLB era, this approach would not be tolerated at most schools. If teachers give high grades on effort, the kids still would have trouble passing tests in English. I like what you said, but I wonder if many teachers in the present climate were able to do this." It is true that in this NCLB era, many schools have to teach to standards rather than to the potential of students. But no matter what the political climate is, we, as educators with conscience and responsibility, should always find ways to reach our students Otherwise, we may lose ourselves and our students by losing our heart and mind in teaching.

The ELLs in this book are beginning ELLs. They have limited English proficiency and are not ready for any tests in English. If teaching them to pass tests becomes the priority in their schooling, teaching and learning will become meaningless to both teachers and students, and struggling students like these ELLs will be driven out of school. A major goal of my efforts in the New York City schools was to implement authentic reading and writing in their literacy instruction for all students—despite their backgrounds and literacy levels. We have encountered a lot of obstacles, and meeting test demands is certainly one of them. However, many teachers in the schools where I worked managed to engage their ELLs with meaningful reading and writing, even in this NCLB era.

Transitional Stages in ELLs' Writing Development

This chapter illustrates two of the four transitional stages in ELLs' writing development: code switching and inter-language. Teaching ELLs who are literate in their first language to write in English involves helping them make transitions from their first-language writing to English. They are writers who need to transfer or apply their knowledge to composing in English. In my work with ELLs, I noticed that code switching and inter-language are typical stages for students moving from their first language to Standard English and that this transition from one stage to another is not linear.

Code-Switching or Mixed-Language Usage

Code-switching, or mixed-language usage, is a common practice among ELLs due to their intensive contact with multiple languages. ELLs live between two worlds, sometimes known as a "borderland" (Anzaldua 1987) where two languages and two cultures come together. They mostly study in English in schools, live in an English-speaking mass-media world, and participate via English in the virtual world. At the same time, they engage in their intimate relationships—with their families, in their communities, and among their friends—using their native language. With bilingual or multilingual contact in their daily lives, code-switching is not only natural, it is unavoidable.

Code-switching is the simultaneous activation of two languages; it is not an accident or the careless language contact of the two incomplete language systems (Grosjean 1989). This practice is common to nonnative English speakers of all ages after they live in the second-language world for a while, no matter what their educational background or level of English proficiency. I have been living in the United States for over twenty years. When I chat with my Chinese friends at a party, at work, or on the phone, we constantly code-switch—automatically and unconsciously. Even when we visit China, we do this habitually. That is why people in China often comment, "those people who come back from America speak in a foreign tone and style—'yang qiang yang diao.'" When visiting China, I have to work very hard not to slip into English while conversing with my families and friends there if I don't want them to feel distanced from me.

After staying with me for a few months in the United States, my parents, who didn't understand a word of English, started code-switching despite having very little contact with the native-English-speaking people outside the home. They continued to do the same for a while even after they went back to China. It was easy for them to use some English words to relate their experience in the this country, using words and phrases such as "party," "yard sale," and "go shopping"—the only regular outings they went on during their stay in the States. I met many old Chinese immigrants during my work in New York City's Chinatown. They had lived in the United States for over half a century in the confines of Chinatown and never learned to speak English. But their dialects were heavily mixed with English words.

This is also the case among bilingual writers. Abby Figueroa, a Spanish-English bilingual author, writes:

I swerve between two languages. I sometimes skirt the edges of proper grammar and social acceptance, and often crash into a linguistic wall. What is that word? Como se dice? And then I remember que lo que you queria decir es muy simplemente expresado en espanol, or may be in English, or may necesito combiner palabras y frases from both languages to get right to the heart, el Corazon de lo que deso explicar. There's something exhilarating about being able to race through una conversacion sin frenando cuando me encuentro trabada and I have the thoughts, the poem, the word at the tip of my tongue just itching to get out but I scrambe por recordarme por la parabra exacta but then I just switch and boom I finished what I had to say and it quite incredibly makes perfect sense. (2004, 286)

Unfortunately, code-switching in writing is not valued in many U.S. schools. It is often considered a sign of deficiency or limited language proficiency in ELLs. Thus, the strategy is discouraged or even forbidden in second-language instruction. Some people think it signals an easy way out for ELLs: instead of working hard to learn new vocabulary or spelling, they code-switch. Some believe that code-switching is first-language interference or language contamination. In order to learn a new language well, the native language should be completely and utterly blocked out. That is why ELLs are forced to think in English when they try to write in English. The myth is that by doing so, the ELLs would write like native-English speakers. This perturbation makes it hard for beginning or intermediate ELLs, especially, as we have noted, those who enter the English-speaking country at the upper elementary and secondary school levels.

Some bilingual educators also oppose the code-switching strategy for language maintenance reasons. At an NCTE conference on bilingual and dual-language education in 2004, Luis Moll, a well-known researcher in bilingual education, stated that in order to practice successful dual-language instruction, English shouldn't be allowed to be used during Spanish instruction, because English, the dominant language, can be too powerful. "If you seal all the windows and doors, it [English] can still sneak into the house to take the place of the language with less power" (Moll 2004). To protect the language of ethnic minority, he recommended forbidding code-switching during Spanish instruction.

I can understand Mr. Moll's reasoning; the same thing occurs in a lot of Chinese American families. In order to maintain their Chinese language, many parents refuse to respond to their children's requests if they don't express them in Chinese (no code-switching allowed). As a result, their children do maintain better Chinese than those who are not disciplined to speak their native language at home. Usually, these children are raised in highly educated bilingual families and the parents consciously put a lot of effort into schooling their children in two languages. But no matter what the strategy adopted for language maintenance is, children constantly code-switch when they speak with peers who share their linguistic background. The truth is, bilinguals use their languages or their hybrid forms with different interlocutors, or different purposes and functions in different domains (Grosjean 1989).

Code-Switching as a Borrowing Strategy

Even though there is some merit to forbidding the use of the code-switching strategies for language acquisition or language maintenance, I believe that in teaching ELLs to write, code-switching is not only a necessary transitional stage, but a useful strategy in promoting the growth of their English writing. When ELLs try to write in English, their thinking is often blocked due to their limited vocabulary. Code-switching can serve as a borrowing strategy by using the native language to fill in the English words they don't know, so they can continue their thinking process. Figure 4.1 shows a beginning ELL's journal entries.

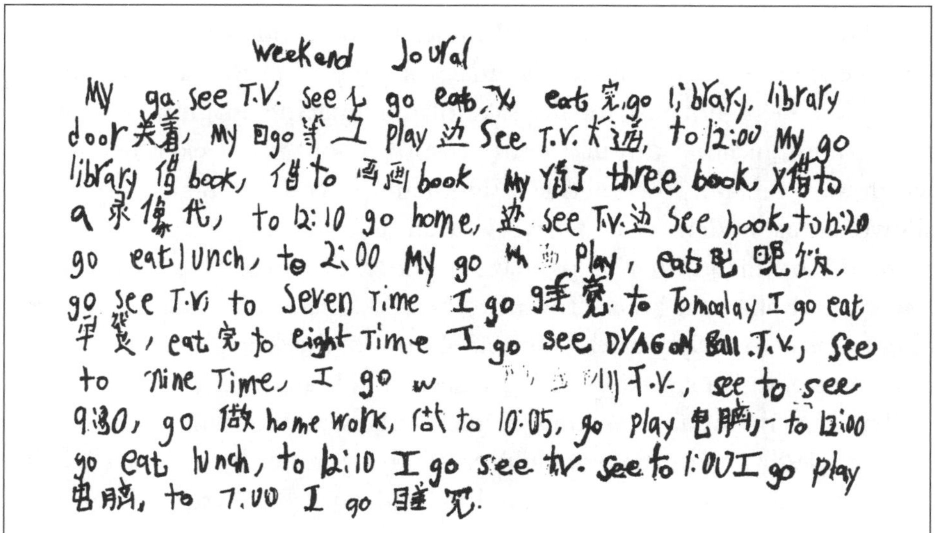

Figure 4.1   *A Beginning ELL's Journal Entries*

This was a weekly journal entry the student wrote to describe what he did during a weekend. He began the journal by saying how he went to the library to get some books, but it was closed. He came home, watched some cartoons on TV while waiting for the library to open. Then he went back to the library and got three picture books and a videotape. During the weekend, he played the computer games, watched TV, did homework, and had good meals. He listed things he did and ended the journal entry with "I went to bed." It was a typical daily journal many ELLs would write. From reading this piece, I can tell that the student didn't have sufficient English language skills to describe what he did during the weekend. But I wondered why he didn't simply write in Chinese. I interviewed him, and here is his response (in Chinese, with my translation):

> This was the work for ESL class. We are supposed to write in English in the ESL class. But I didn't know a lot of English words or say things in English, so I used Chinese, this way I could tell about my weekend life. If I didn't use the Chinese, I couldn't tell about what I did during my weekend. If I wrote in Chinese, the ESL teacher couldn't read my writing. When I mixed the languages, I could tell everything I did. I think my teacher should be able to understand some, if not all.

From what this student expressed I understood his purpose for describing his weekend. In using mixed-language strategy for this assignment he wrote this piece not just for the sake of fulfilling the assignment, but for truly communicating through written words about his weekend activities, which was the purpose of the assignment. If code-switching were not allowed, this student would have written as much as his English ability allowed, and his journal might have sounded like this: "I go see TV, go library, go home, eat lunch. I went to bed." Code-switching gave him the opportunity to fully express himself. I found the same practice among beginning Spanish-speaking ELLs, as shown in Figure 4.2.

The mixed-language writing of these ELLs reminds me of how Jane Hansen (1987) contrasts two children's writing in her book *When Writers Read*: one child wrote in neat English, and one child wrote in invented spelling.

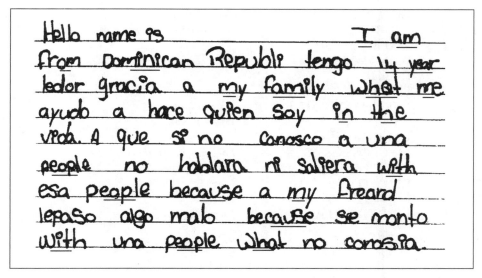

Figure 4.2 *Code-Switching in Beginning Spanish-Speaking ELLs*

Suzanne's work:

> My name is Suzanne.
> I am six years old.
> I go to school.
> I have a dog.

Daniel's work:

(Original)	(Translation)
WEN RAN	*When rain comes down*
KUMS DAN	
IT DANS	*It dances in the puddles*
IS IN THU PUDLES	
AND	*And splashes in the air.*
SPLAZI IN THU	
IR PSSSSS	*p-s-s-s-s-s.*
IT SPASHI	*It splashes on the window*
ON THU WIND	

GOO PAT PAT PAT	*Goes "Pat, pat, pat"*
IND I KENS	*And I catch it in my mouth.*
IND MY MUSH	
WEN I WOK	*When I walk in the puddles*
IN THU	
UDLS	
I TRI TO SPLASH T	*I try to splash it*
WEND I K	*When I come home*
UM HOM	
I ?? CLOSSSSSSS	*I change my clothes-s-s-s-s-s*
I LUV I	*I love it*
I LUV IT	*I love it*
I LUV IT	*I love it*
I LUV THU RAN	*I love the rain.*

(12)

This contrast demonstrates that when ELLs like these two children are forced to use only the limited English proficiency they have, the writing can be pedestrian and flat, but if allowed to use their own language to express themselves, they can write vivid pieces.

Code-Switching as Bilingual Expression

For ELL writers, code-switching may serve as a borrowing strategy, but this is not always the case. ELLs may choose to mix languages for other reasons: for convenience, for accuracy, or for cultural expressions. For instance, the word *shopping* in English has a broader meaning than its Chinese counterpart. It includes window shopping, grocery shopping, or shopping in a mall. In Chinese, each activity has a different phrase: window shopping/(walking on the street—*guang jie*), or grocery shopping (going to the market—*shang cai chang*), and shopping in the mall (going to a department store—*guang shang dian*). It is easier to use the English phrase "go shopping" than the corresponding Chinese expressions. Other groups of words, such as *uncle*, *aunt*, *in-laws*, *social studies*, and *science class* are also much more generic in English than in Chinese. Chinese has at least half a dozen words for the English word *uncle*. And in China, there are three different courses (history, geography, and politics) that are all categorized under social studies in the States. So when Chinese-speaking ELLs talk about their social studies class, they would simply use "social studies" since there is no equivalent phrase for a class like social studies in the schools in China.

Also, while studying English, ELLs are learning a lot of new concepts. Among them, they learned some in English for the first time such as condo, download, and sex; and some are totally new concepts that have no equivalent in Chinese, such as garage or yard sale, layaway, or the Projects (a public apartment building for low-income families). When ELLs express ideas associated with these concepts, it is much easier and more convenient to use the English words. Similarly, when ELLs become proficient English speakers, they tend to use a lot of words from their native language in their English speech—certain expressions that are either untranslatable or would lose their unique flavor, intimacy, or accuracy through translation. Code-switching is a signature of being bilingual and evidence of living a life between two linguistic and cultural worlds.

Code-switching is not just an oral language practice among bilinguals, but a practice often adopted by bilingual writers to show their emotion and identity. In a summer institute for teachers, all the participants wrote and shared their writing every day. Many bilingual teachers used both their native language and English to compose. Some started with English and ended in their native language; some started and ended their writing in English, and wrote the middle in their native language. Here is an excerpt of a piece written by a Spanish-speaking teacher:

She started her piece in English and ended in Spanish:

I'm from Mexico. A place of beautiful culture and interesting history. A place of thousand of small town with weird name and sometimes difficult to pronounce. I can say that I'm from Amatepetlan. I lived here my first five years. It is my grandparents Rancho or farm. I loved this place the history and the roots of my family. I love the mountains, the trees, birds and the river of Amatepetlan. . . .

Razones que justifican tido los mas jovernes no saben par que. Yo si se.Ocurria una desgracia si y siempre foe secreto. Los jovenes no teniamos derecho a enterurms de los conflictos aguntos delicardos. Si muy delicardis de vida o mverte. Para protejernej major era no saber nada.

When asked why she code-switched in her writing, this teacher replied, "I started to write in English, and then I got very emotional and switched to write in Spanish. It is easier to use Spanish to express my emotion. Spanish to me is more musical. I tend to do professional writing in English and express my deep feelings in Spanish." This teacher was consciously code-switching to reach deep into her emotions.

Abby Figueroa loves to express her thoughts about being bilingual with mixed-language expressions:

> With two ways to say everything I'm hardly at a disadvantage. How I speak Spanish and English is a reflection of the culture I live everyday. And unless there's something wrong with my almost bilingual and very bicultural life, then there's nothing wrong with combining the two languages I grew up with. Yo hablare en dos idomas as long I can think in two. (2004, 286)

I found many ELLs at intermediate or advanced level in the middle schools who presented themselves in a similar way, through writing in mixed languages, though they are not so consciously aware of this feat as these adult writers are.

Code-Switching as Practice Using English in a Meaningful Context

When code-switching became accepted practice for ELLs' writing in our schools, beginning ELLs not only were less frustrated with their writing, but also enjoyed mixing English words and phrases with their native-language writing. To them, this was a meaningful way to utilize newly learned English vocabulary in the context of their writing, a more effective way to learn language skills than filling in the blanks on worksheets, making sentences, or taking spelling tests. In the New York City's Chinatown schools, the ELLs started writing in their native language on the first day of class, but they were encouraged in their ESL class to use as much English as they could in their writing. Betty, the ESL teacher at Dr. Sun Yat Sen Middle School, expressed her strong belief that this was the way for her ELLs to practice using English words and skills in the context of writing. She pushed her students to use English from their first week of writing (see

Figure 4.3). The ELLs are also encouraged to code-switch in their bilingual social studies class, where the native language is the dominant language in teaching and learning—a practice many bilingual educators oppose. Based on my understanding of the ELLs' living situation in New York City's Chinatown, I hold a different view from those bilingual educators (see *An Island of English: Teaching ESL in Chinatown* [Fu 2003]). I strongly support helping ELLs build their academic English vocabulary and skills while teaching them content knowledge in their native language.

The beginning ELLs at Dr. Sun Yat Sen Middle School all took bilingual classes where they were studying content knowledge in Chinese. As the research indicates, it takes five to seven or more years for ELLs to acquire academic English (Cummins 1981; Thomas and Collier 1997). Consequently, the school leadership team consisting of faculty, school administrators, and staff developers decided to introduce academic English vocabulary into content study so that the ELLs could develop those skills along with their native language skills. In the bilingual social studies class, students studied American history, geography, and government. The main textbook was written in Chinese, but many English-written

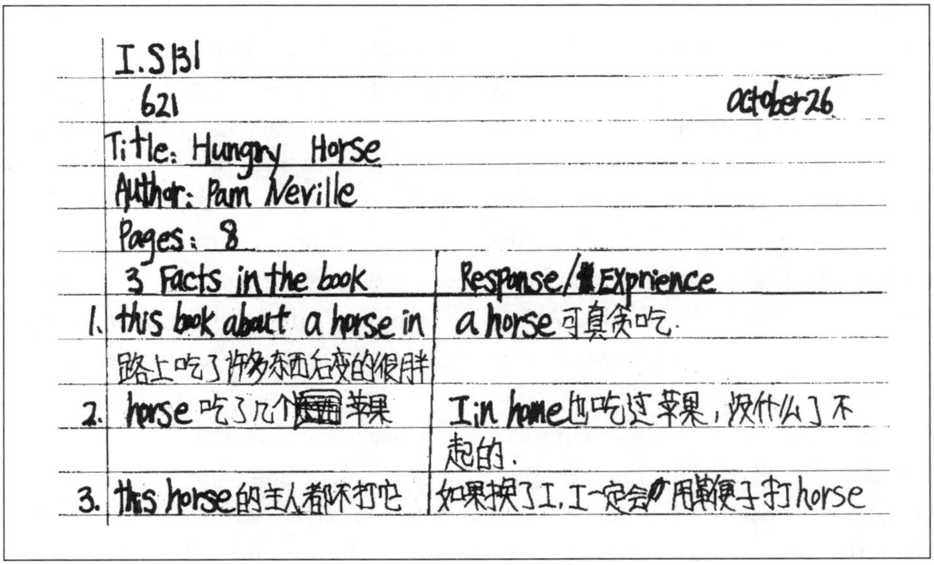

Figure 4.3 *Reading Response Mixed with Chinese Words*

picture books on various topics were used as supplemental and independent reading sources in class or for self-selected homework reading. The teachers taught lessons in Chinese, but introduced terminology in English.

Every week, the students learned a social studies topic with content-related English vocabulary. Since the focus of the class was the content, there was no special spelling instruction for English vocabulary. Students had weekly writing assignments on the topics they learned. Code-switching was acceptable but not required for writing. Many students chose to mix English words into their Chinese writing, saying, "If we don't use them, we won't remember them." The ESL teachers found that their ELLs developed quite impressive vocabularies in their bilingual social studies class, which was very helpful when, as they remarked, "our class[es] started to read books on the social studies topics such as American Indians, immigrants, and American presidents. They not only have the knowledge base of the American history, but also have some English vocabulary to start reading the English books."

In the ESL classes, students were allowed to write in their native language, but once they learned some English—either individual words, phrases, or some simple sentences—they were encouraged to employ them in their writing. Their teachers welcomed the use of English words and phrases in the ELLs' first-language-dominant writing and accepted code-switching or the mixed usage of both languages. They believed this not only helped students hone their English language skills, but also encouraged the development of the social, cognitive, and linguistic flexibility associated with bilingualism as Abby Figueroa states: "I'd usually butcher the grammar in both languages and grapple for that exact word I wanted" (2004, 284). Like Abby, ELLs would employ bilingual sources to express themselves, rather than stick to grammar rules in either one language.

I interviewed a dozen teachers in my study about how they viewed their students' different language usages in writing, especially the ELLs' mixed-language writing. Most of the teachers said that they had no problem with any language their students used to write: The bilingual teachers were wide open to any language their students chose to use for their writing as long as they presented their ideas in full. The ESL teachers were not used to reading the mixed-language writing, but grew to like it because the students' mixed-language writing gave them clues about what language skills they needed to teach in order for the students to express themselves. As Betty said, "I push them to use as much English as possible, so they would make transitions to English writing. To me, mixed language is only a transitional stage, and they can't stay in this stage forever." Because ELLs were allowed to write in their native language in both ESL and bilingual classes, they not only learned new concepts, content knowledge, and English skills, but also utilized code-switching strategies to practice their learned English vocabulary in writing in both classes. Because of the different focuses in bilingual classes (content knowledge) and ESL classes (language skills), students had the freedom to code-switch when they wrote for bilingual class but were pushed to make progressive transitions to English writing in the ESL class.

According to New York State policy on bilingual and ESL education, transitional bilingual programs should start the school year using the students' native language, which should gradually decrease, as more and more English is used. In the ESL program, the policy recommends "English only." Our ESL teachers felt tremendous pressure to push their students to make transitions in their writing development from their native language to English, though they sometimes felt, as one teacher stated, "my push may put too much emphasis on the students' language learning rather than their true expression" in their writing. In any case, code-switching practice is valued and is seen as a useful and necessary stage in ELL writing development in most of the schools I worked in. Just as it is a common practice among all nonnative English speakers, code-switching or mixed-language usage was a common practice in our ELLs' writing. James Alatis (2005), a well-known linguist from Georgetown University, proposed that the objective of English teaching should be to enable students "to switch codes instinctively and to communicate in the most appropriate language or dialect, in a manner most conductive to producing the greatest amount of cooperation and the least amount of resistance" (32).

Inter-Language

Stage 3, inter-language, also reflects a natural developmental stage as ELLs learn to speak and write in English. A typical characteristic of beginning ELLs' inter-language writing is using English words in the syntax of their native language. The following are examples of inter-language writing: the first written by a Spanish-speaking ELL and the second written by a Chinese-speaking ELL. Both pieces are about special persons in their lives.

My Family
My family. I has one father, one Mother, and I sister. Every body in my family are special but someone special is my mother. She make me a new life. She help me all my life. She is a good women and she is a special women. She know everything about family. Everybody told me "your mother is a smart girl" I feel very proud about my mother.

My Best Friend
I have a very Friend. He of no tall, hair long, mouth very small, eyes is of small. He in go home time and I together do we homework. Sometimes we together play. Sometimes we together go to school. He is my best friend.

The piece in Figure 4.4 was written by a Spanish-speaking boy about a summer event he experienced.

At this stage, ELLs think mostly in their native language while trying to speak or write in English. Therefore, their English expression is either directly translated from their native language or strongly influenced by it. ELLs' inter-language speaking and writing can sound very foreign to monolingual English speakers. It is commonly seen as "broken English" by the general public. Although all language learners go through this stage in their second-language acquisition, some view it as first-language interference.

ELLs' inter-language writing, packed with ungrammatical sentences and unidiomatic expressions, irritates and frustrates many teachers, who say, "I don't know even how to start to correct their writing. I almost have to rewrite every sentence of their work to get it to sound right. . . ." I have heard this kind of frustration voiced at every grade level, from elementary

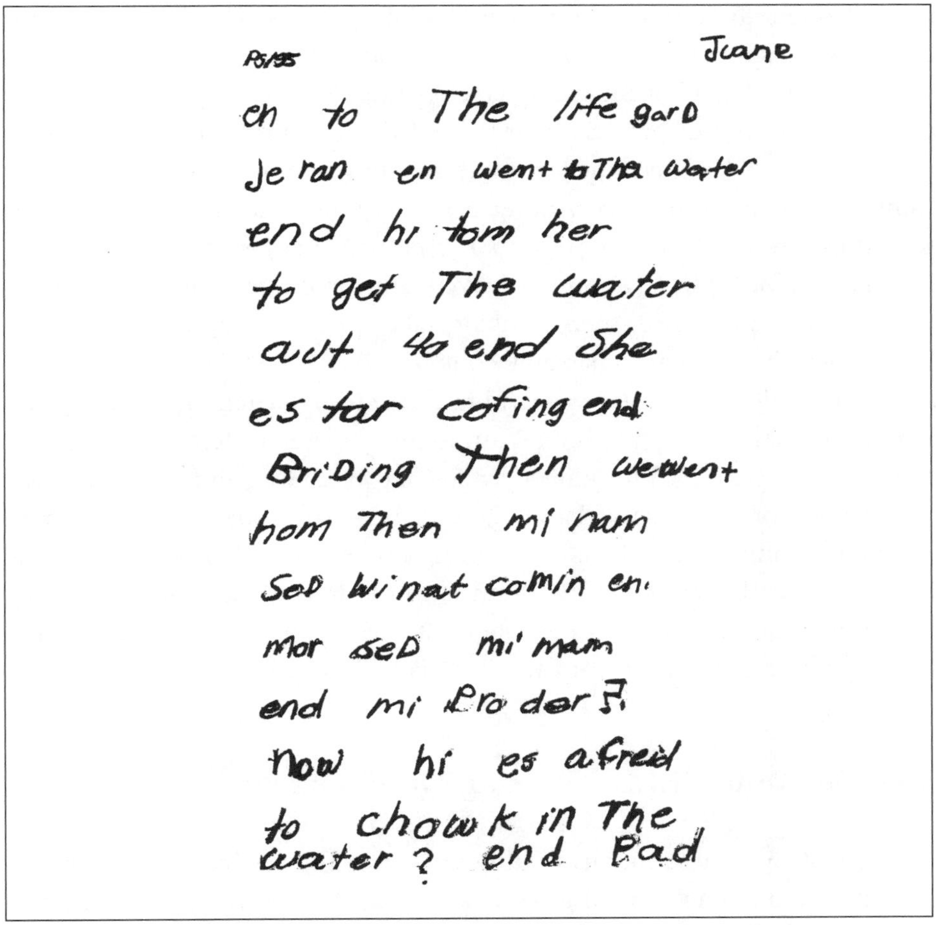
PS/35 Juane

en to The life garD
Je ran en went to Tha water
end hi tom her
to get The water
aut to end She
es tar cofing end
BriDing Then wewent
hom Then mi mam
SeD winat comin en.
mor seD mi mam
end mi Broder 7.
now hi es afreid
to chowk in The
water? end Bad

Figure 4.4 *A Piece Written by a Spanish-Speaking Boy About a Summer Event He Experienced*

school to graduate school. Inter-language writing is not produced solely by beginning ELLs, but by ELLs at all levels, depending on the topic and kind of writing they do. Advanced-level ELLs may be able to express themselves in English fluently when they talk about their everyday life experiences or discuss certain familiar topics in their field of study. But when they have to use English to describe unfamiliar or complicated academic themes or explain something they learned only in their native language, their English expression will be colored by native-language features and will sound unidiomatic to native-English speakers. This happens to my own English speaking and writing all the time.

To avoid producing inter-language writing, ELLs are often pushed to think in English, but because their limited English proficiency can't match their thinking, it is like using a toy axe to chop a big tree. To be forced to think only in English when writing not only limits the language available to express an idea but also prevents the human brain from functioning at its fullest; it is, actually, impossible. We can't force our brains to choose a language to think in. Rather, thinking takes place through any language with which the brain automatically connects. As Qi (1998) discussed in his study on students' language switching, "language-switching [takes] place as if it were enacted by a force of automaticity" (420). Before ELLs reach the level of certain or full English proficiency in reading and speaking, they have to rely on their native language to think—to produce, shape, generate, and organize their ideas. The writing process for ELLs involves translation. For ELL beginners, this translation is frequently word for word, which may sound "broken," especially when the syntax of the ELLs' native language is very different from English, like Chinese is.

Two Beginning ELLs' Writing Development

When ELLs were able to start writing as soon as they arrived in our schools and allowed and encouraged to code-switch in their writing, I noticed that they developed rapidly as writers, with less frustration and less resistance in expressing themselves in English than students in "English-only" environments. The following two cases illustrate my findings. These two students were both first-year ELLs at Dr. Sun Yat Sen Middle School. Jing arrived in the United States a month before school started; Ming came to the country in late September and nine days later enrolled as a student in this Chinatown school. On their first day of the school, their ESL teacher, Betty, asked them to do a writing assignment on a self-chosen topic, written in their first language but using as much English as they could. The purpose of this assignment was to assess where their literacy level was and how much English they knew. Jing wrote the piece shown in Figure 4.5.

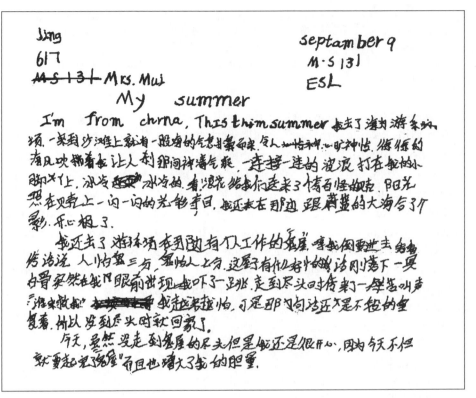

Figure 4.5 *Jing's Assignment*

Here is the translation:

I am from China. This is my summer. I went to a seaside Fair Land. When we were approaching the sea shore, a fresh smell of the ocean came into our lungs, energizing our bodies, and we were wakened up by the soft sea breeze. Waves upon waves padded my small feet, so cold. The waves sent us varying kinds of sea shells, blinking under the sunshine, with multi eye-catching colors. I took a picture with the big blue ocean at the back, how exciting.

I also went to the man-made "Haunted House." "Hm . . ." I thought to myself, "I want to go in as we often say: 'Ghosts are scared of humans three times more than the humans of the ghosts.' And only a house, how scaring would this be?!" Just as I thought of this, a skeleton jumped right in front of my face, which almost took my breath away. Approaching to the dead end, I heard a repeating weepy cry "Help! Help!" I got more and more scared with nonstop crying howl. I turned back and quit the journey.

Today, I had a great time, though I didn't complete my tour of the Haunted House, for I not only saw a haunted house, but also I found I was quite brave.

Jing was quite a good writer in his native language: he had good organization skills, added intricate details, and concluded the piece with a self-realization. In addition to this writing assignment, Betty asked him to read a dozen sight words (such as *dog, cat, desk, green, red*), a few of which he could recognize.

For the same assignment, Ming wrote in Chinese. His version was much shorter and simpler than Jing's. When he received the assignment, he expressed that he didn't know what to write. So Betty told him, "Why not just tell me about yourself?" He copied Betty's word *myself* and wrote the piece in Figure 4.6. After Betty conferred with him and said, "You should first tell me what your name is," he added his name.

Here is the translation:

My name is Ming. I am in the sixth grade. My father and I came to America and my mother is still at home in China. My grandpa and grandma are in America too. I came from China.

Figure 4.6 *Ming's Assignment*

His Chinese writing was below sixth-grade level, The only English he could write was his name, which is the same as Chinese Pingying (Chinese phonics used for pronunciation). On the sight-word exercise, the only two words he could recognize were *dog* and *cat*. Jing and Ming were both at a nonproficient English level.

Betty taught all beginning ELLs. In her class, students wrote every day, with journal writing and reading responses as daily writing activities. Students would respond to pictures when they couldn't understand the words in the picture books they read. They would tell stories from reading the pictures. Betty let her students write in their native language as often as they needed to but pushed them to use English words she knew they had learned, as shown in the example in Figure 4.7: Betty knew this student learned the word *I*, and she pointed it out in her response.

She explains her practice here:

> This is ESL class. In this class, they are supposed to develop their English language skills. I let them use Chinese as the transition, but I don't want them to stay in their native language. I want them to use every opportunity to practice using the English words and skills they learned in the context of reading and writing, otherwise, how can they build their skills fast enough?

Within one year, all of Betty's students, no matter at what level they started out, made obvious progress in their writing development.

Let's look at the progress Jing and Ming made respectively in Betty's class. Figure 4.8 shows one of Jing's November journal entries after spending two and a half months in Betty's class.

In this piece, Jing talked about getting ready for his first Thanksgiving in the United States. In the art class, he was making paper turkeys. He made twenty-one turkeys and colored their wings, but by accident, he cut off one of the wings, so one turkey was wounded and couldn't fly any more. He said the turkeys he made were beautiful, but were only for display, and not for food. He concluded this piece with a bed-to-bed format: I got home, took a bath, did home work, ate dinner, and "go to bed and close eyes." Obviously he was learning more English, though he still couldn't express himself completely in English.

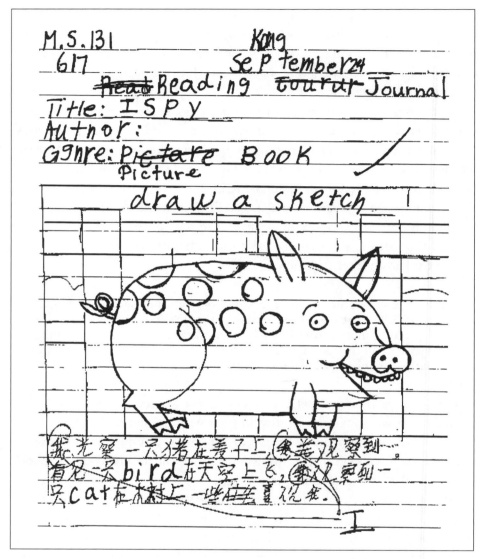

M.S. 131   Kong
617   September 24
~~Read~~ Reading ~~tourar~~ Journal
Title: I S P Y
Author:
Genre: ~~Pictate~~ B O O K   ✓
          Picture

draw a sketch

我先察 一只猪着在养子上,(我差观察到.
有只一只 bird 在天空上飞,我又察到一
只 cat 在树上 一些由差喜记我.   I

Figure 4.7   *Kong's Reading Journal*

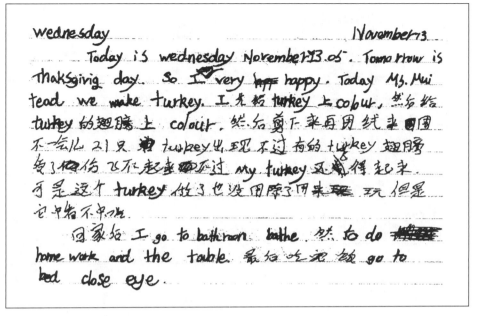

Figure 4.8 *Jing's Writing Progress (November)*

Figure 4.9 shows one of Ming's journal entries from December, also two months from when he arrived in Betty's class.

This is what he wrote:

Today is Tuesday, December 20th, 2005. This morning I watch TV. TV says that today no car (subway workers strike). I then stayed home sleep until 10:00 when the school started. Mrs Yu was absent, so we had a sub teacher. The sub teacher told us we could do anything we want to as long as we don't make too much noise. I did all my home work in class. After school, I went to library with Jia Yu, where we applied for library card and then we went to play computer game. We play CS till 6:00 and we went home.

I can tell he tried arduously to express himself in English though he still had very limited English skills. He didn't know how to say, "library card" so he wrote, "the card of the books." That is a very clever way to use the

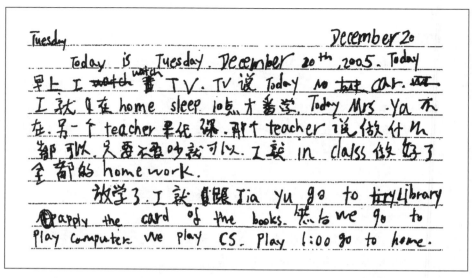

Figure 4.9   *Ming's Writing Progress (December)*

words he knew to express the meaning he tried to convey. He came to Betty's class with below-grade-level Chinese-writing skills. By practicing every day, his writing became longer and included more details.

Let's look at another two pieces written by these two students after they had studied in Betty's class for four months (see Figures 4.10 and 4.11). Figure 4.10 is by Jing, from one of his journals in January, and Figure 4.11 is by Ming, from one of his journals in February.

After four months of learning English through reading and writing (talking is a big part too) every day in Betty's class, these two students were able to express their daily activities and lives mostly in English. Jing had a few Chinese words dotted in his writing (two phrases: dynasties and long history), and Ming still used many Chinese words. Comparing these two pieces written by Jing and Ming, I found that Ming's writing described more complex activities than the simple activities listed by Jing in his journal. Ming's writing mentions the parent-teacher conference he took his father to attend, and talks about how they had many visitors to his class one day, and how he felt about being observed by so many teachers— "I was so nervous that I was afraid to say something wrong in front of so

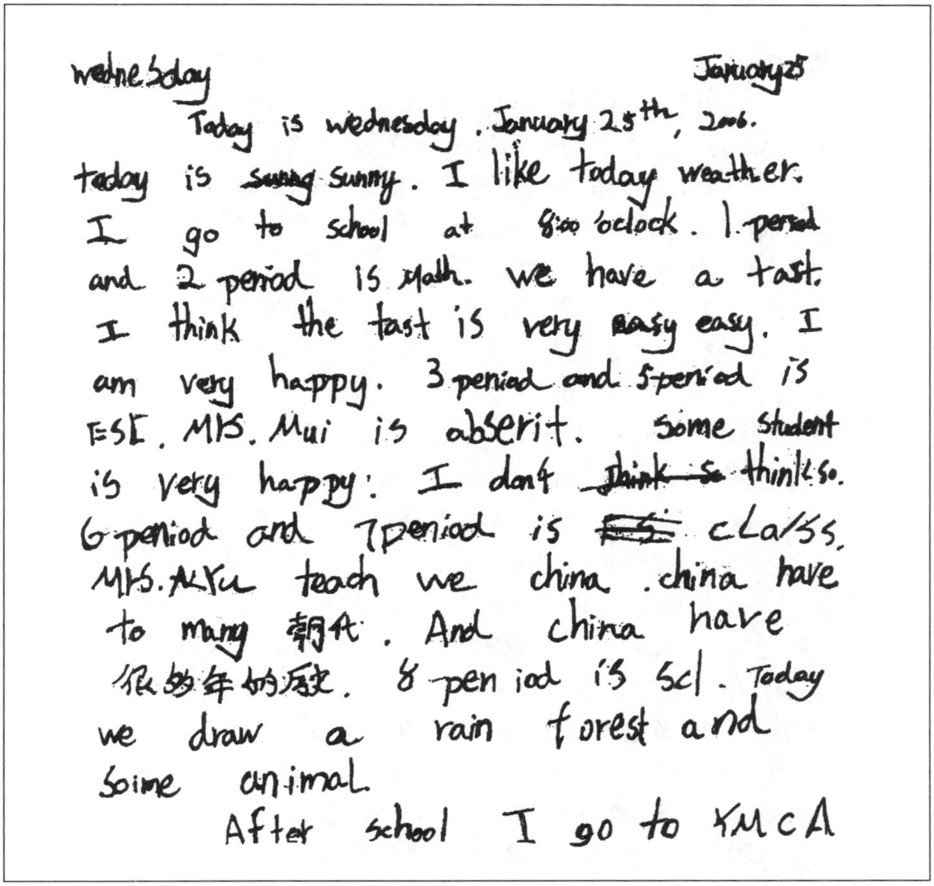

wedneSday January25

Today is wednesday. January 25th, 2006. today is ~~sunng~~ sunny. I like today weather. I go to school at 8:00 o'clock. 1 period and 2 period is Math. we have a tast. I think the tast is very ~~easy~~ easy. I am very happy. 3 peniad and 5 periad is ESL. MRS. Mui is abserit. some student is very happy: I dont ~~think so~~ think so. 6 peniod and 7 peniod is ~~ESL~~ class. MRS. AKu teach we china. china have to many 朝代. And china have 很多年的历史. 8 pen iod is Scl. Today we draw a rain forest and some animal.

After school I go to YMCA

Figure 4.10 *Jing's Writing Progress (February)*

many teachers." Then he described the basketball game he played with his friends: who made the teams, who won, who brought drinks and, later, how two black boys joined them to play basketball, and his team won. Compared with how reluctant he was to write when he first came to Betty, four months later he had made a tremendous leap as a writer. He chose important events to describe rather than merely listing the menial routine tasks that happened from morning to evening, and his writing was rich with details. Undoubtedly, if he was not allowed to code-switch (using mixed languages), he wouldn't be able to express himself to this degree.

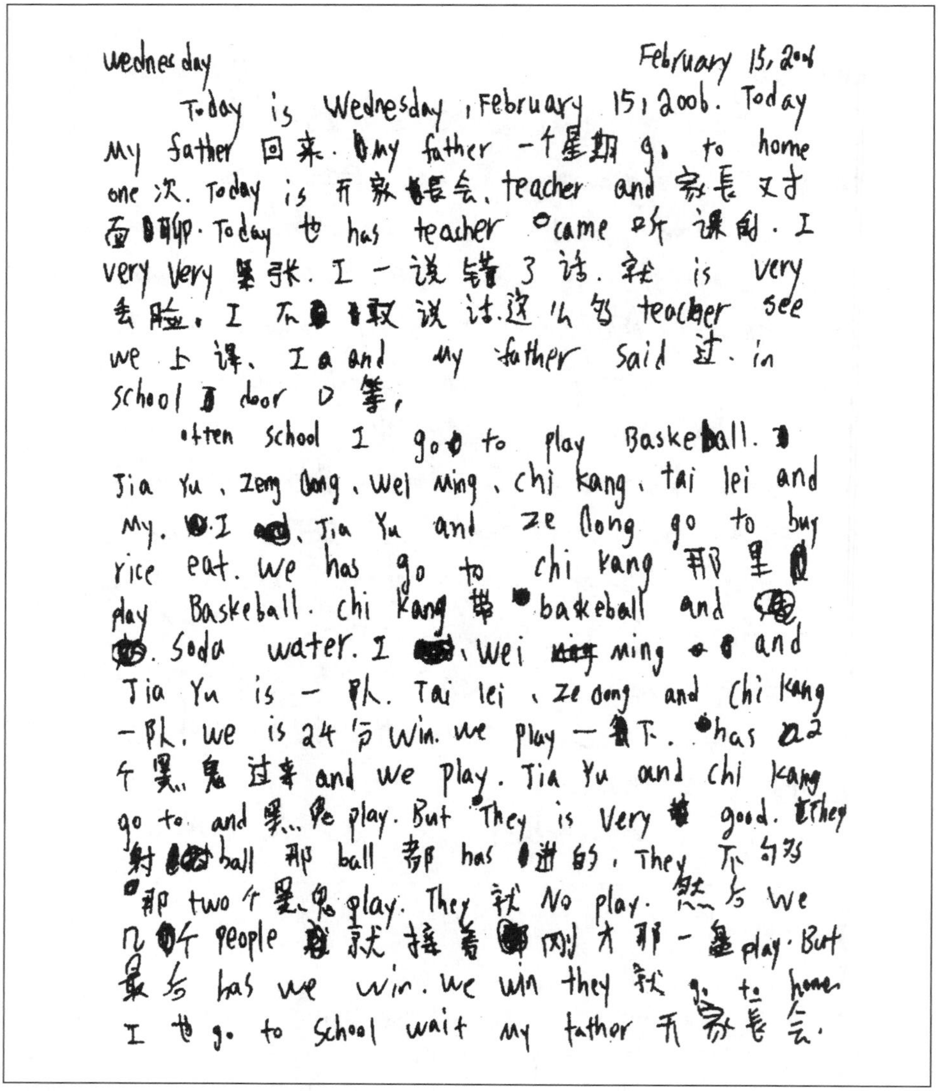

wednesday   February 15, 2006

Today is Wednesday, February 15, 2006. Today
My father 回来. My father 一个星期 go to home
one 次. Today is 开家长会, teacher and 家长又对
面的啊. Today 也 has teacher came 听课的. I
very very 紧张. I 一说错了话. 就 is very
丢脸. I 不敢说话这么多 teacher see
we 上课. I a and my father said 过. in
school 的 door 口等.

often school I go to play Basketball.
Jia yu, Zeng dong, Wei ming, chi kang, tai lei and
My. I, Jia Yu and ze long go to buy
rice eat. we has go to chi kang 那里
play Basketball. chi kang bakeball and
soda water. I, Wei ming and
Jia Yu is 一队. Tai lei, Ze dong and chi kang
一队. we is 24 分 win. we play 一下. has 2个
个黑鬼过来 and we play. Jia Yu and chi kang
go to and 黑. we play. But They is very good. they
射 ball 那 ball 都 has 进的. They 不知为
那 two 个黑鬼 play. They 就 No play. 然后 we
几个 people 就接着刚才那一起 play. But
最后 has we win. we win they 就 go to home.
I 也 go to school wait my father 开家长会.

Figure 4.11   *Ming's Writing Progress (December)*

In March, six months after Jing started in Betty's class, his journal
writing was all in English at a comprehensible level. See the example in
Figure 4.12.

The main idea of this piece is that it was a Sunday, and it was raining
outside so he had to stay inside. He got so bored and killed a mouse. The

writing shows he was at the inter-language stage (Stage 3) as a writer in English.

In March, after learning in Betty's class for five months, Ming also could express his daily experiences mostly in English, and his writing is still interspersed with Chinese words (see Figure 4.13).

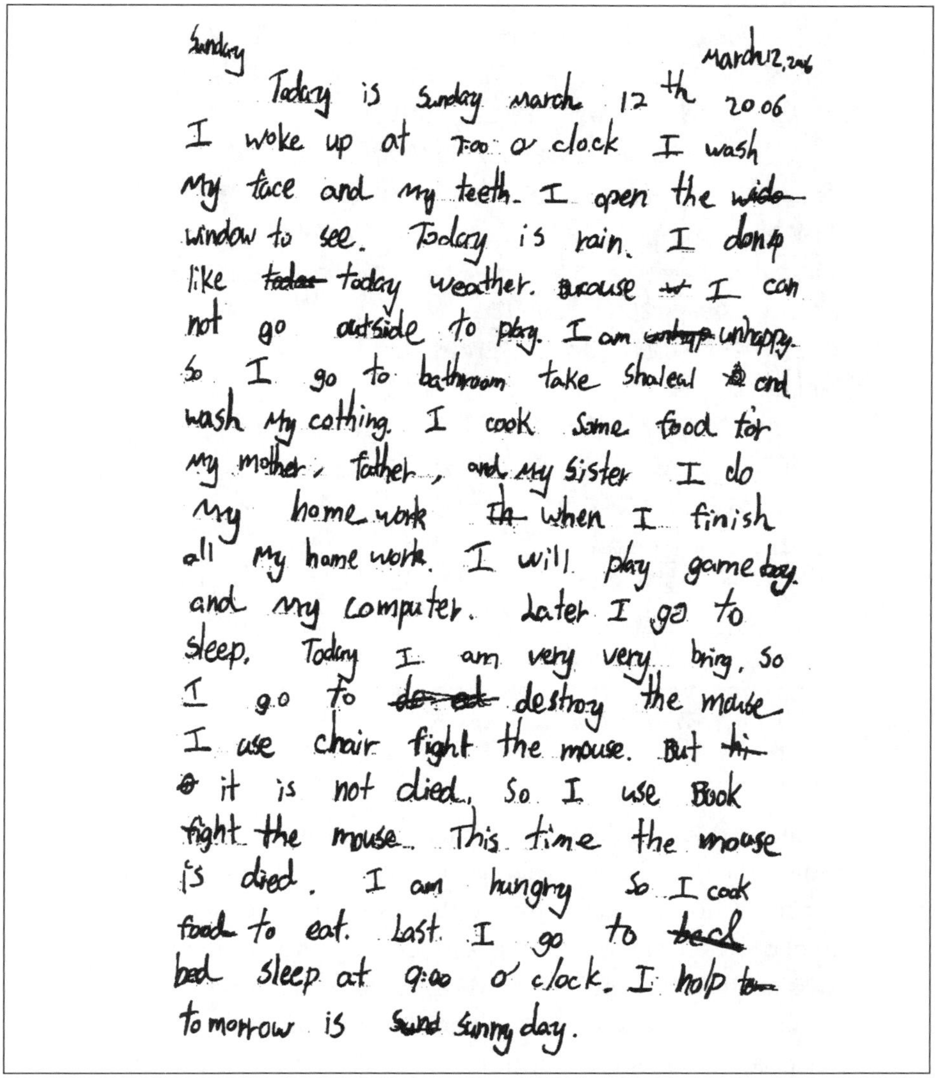
Sunday March 12, 2006
Today is Sunday march 12 th 20.06
I woke up at 7:00 o clock I wash
My face and my teeth. I open the ~~wido~~
window to see. Today is rain. I donp
like ~~todar~~ today weather. ~~because~~ ~~w~~ I can
not go outside to play. I am ~~unhap~~ unhappy.
So I go to bathroom take Shaleal ~~a~~ and
wash My cothing. I cook Some food for
my mother, father, and my sister I do
my home work ~~th~~ when I finish
all my home work. I will play game boy
and my computer. Later I go to
sleep. Today I am very very bring. So
I go to ~~do eat~~ destroy the mouse
I use chair fight the mouse. But ~~hi~~
~~e~~ it is not died. So I use Book
fight the mouse. This time the mouse
is died. I am hungry So I cook
food to eat. Last I go to ~~bed~~
bed sleep at 9:00 o'clock. I holp ~~to~~
tomorrow is ~~Sund~~ Sunny day.

Figure 4.12 *Jing's Writing Progress (March)*

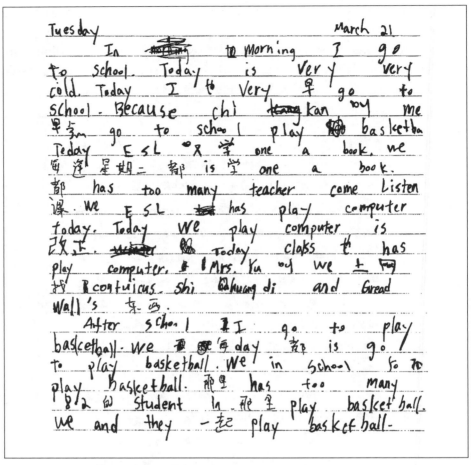

Figure 4.13   *Ming's Writing Progress (March)*

In this piece, Ming talked about what he did in his ESL and bilingual social studies class, and about his friends and his playing basketball with them after the school. Clearly, his English is improving in terms of grammar, sentence structure, vocabulary, and spelling after studying English for five months in Betty's room. Since Ming came to Betty with below-grade-level first-language literacy, it is especially encouraging to see how he developed certain fluency in writing. From reading the collection of his journal writing, I can tell that, rather than writing in a manner like laying bricks, struggling to produce each word and sentence, he wrote whatever came to his mind and traveled freely between two languages to express himself through written words.

In tracing the development of these two beginning ELL writers during their first year in Betty's class, I am able to identify the four obvious transitional stages introduced earlier in the book (native language, code-switching, inter-language, and conventional English) in their development from writing in their native language to English. These two students had different levels of first-language literacy when they started their school in the United States. They both made the steady and smooth transition into English writing in terms of using written languages to express their daily experiences and activities. Ming's growth as a writer was indeed a surprise to me. He came to Betty's class with first-language literacy that was probably three years below his sixth-grade level. Within one year in an American school, he had gained English proficiency. He was able to express his daily life experiences through written languages because he was required to write every day and given the linguistic freedom to travel between languages. The fluency shown and the ideas expressed in his journal writing definitely demonstrate his growth as a writer. Jing came to Betty's class as a strong writer in his first language. He experienced no difficulty producing a pretty impressive piece in Chinese on the spot. By the end of year in Betty's class, he was able to express himself through journal writing quite fluently with close to conventional English. His obvious growth was in his English proficiency, from barely knowing a few English words to being able to describe his daily life activities solely in English. In terms of his progress as a writer, his English writing had not reached a skill level that would allow him to do what he could in his native language. None of the pieces he wrote in English that year had the sophistication of the piece entitled, "My Summer," which he produced on the first day of school. Jing progressed as an English language learner, but did not quite develop fully as a writer within one year in an American school. This is quite typical for ELLs who come to us as strong writers in their native language. It takes years before their English proficiency parallels their native-language literacy, especially when the students are older (beyond upper elementary level).

Nonlinear Progress in Writing Development

The writing development shown in Jing's and Ming's journal writing offers a general picture of how ELLs progress in their English writing. Their journal-writing examples, which mainly describe their daily school and life experiences, indicate their steady and smooth transition from writing in their native language to English. For this type of writing, ELLs use communicative language, which resembles everyday speech and is less formal and dense than academic writing. The fairly orderly transition shown in this communicative writing doesn't happen when ELLs are engaged in the more academic writing associated with content learning. This transition from one stage to another does not always progress linearly, even in the ELLs' journal writing, because it depends on what topics they choose to write about, what audience they want to speak to, and in which genre they decide to write. Laman and Sluys (2008) posit, "The multilingual children's writing practice of choosing languages calls us to consider kinds of writing opportunities we provide where children are enabled and valued for traversing the territories of their multiple languages" (272).

Rather than moving linearly, ELLs' writing development follows the writing process itself, which involves stages of prewriting or rehearsal, drafting, revising, editing, and finalizing (publishing), but usually doesn't happen in this order. A natural writing process is more recursive than linear; it moves back and forth, and eventually reaches the end-publishing or presentable stage. I found this to be true with ELLs' writing development from their native language to English.

When I looked over students' writing portfolios, I also found this nonlinear pattern of writing development. Among the selected work in the portfolios, collected throughout the year and arranged from the beginning to the end, some early work was written in English, but much later work was written in Chinese because the later presentations were more academic than the earlier ones, which were either narratives of how they spent their summer or descriptions of what they had studied in the previous school year. Let's examine two examples from one student's portfolio work for the bilingual social studies class (see Figures 4.14 and 4.15). Figure 4.14 was written at the beginning of the school year.

I. 5. 131
718

Zhao

Classwork #1

What Did I Learn In 6 Grade S.S. Class

In 6 Grade, I learn reading in Ms. O'keffe's class. Ms. O'keffe gave us book to read and copy down the book. Them Ms. O'keffe asked us some question about that book. After that, she let us to find the ruyming word from the book Then, she let us read the book to her. I learn English in Miss Feng's class. She also gave us story books to read. She read the book for us one time, and then we read the book to her. After that, she let us to do a Sensational Sociogram about the book And then we made a Sensational Sociogram about ourself. Then, we wrote down the word we got trouble to read and don't understand that word's meaning. Then, we need to write from memory the word.

Figure 4.14 *Writing Portfolio from the Beginning of the School Year*

In Figure 4.14, the student demonstrated her adequate English proficiency: good spelling, sentence structure, and vocabulary with no code-switching. From this piece of writing, we can ascertain that the student has reached Stage 4 in her writing development—close to Standard English. But the piece in Figure 4.15, written three weeks later, was switched to Chinese-dominant writing mixed with some English words.

This piece was a summary of what was learned during the week about the American Indians. Compared with Figure 4.14, this piece is more academically oriented, packed with information, and laced with content-specific vocabulary. In responding to the questions asked by the teacher in English, this student chose to write in Chinese mixed with a few terminologies and nouns in English. In presenting the content knowledge she

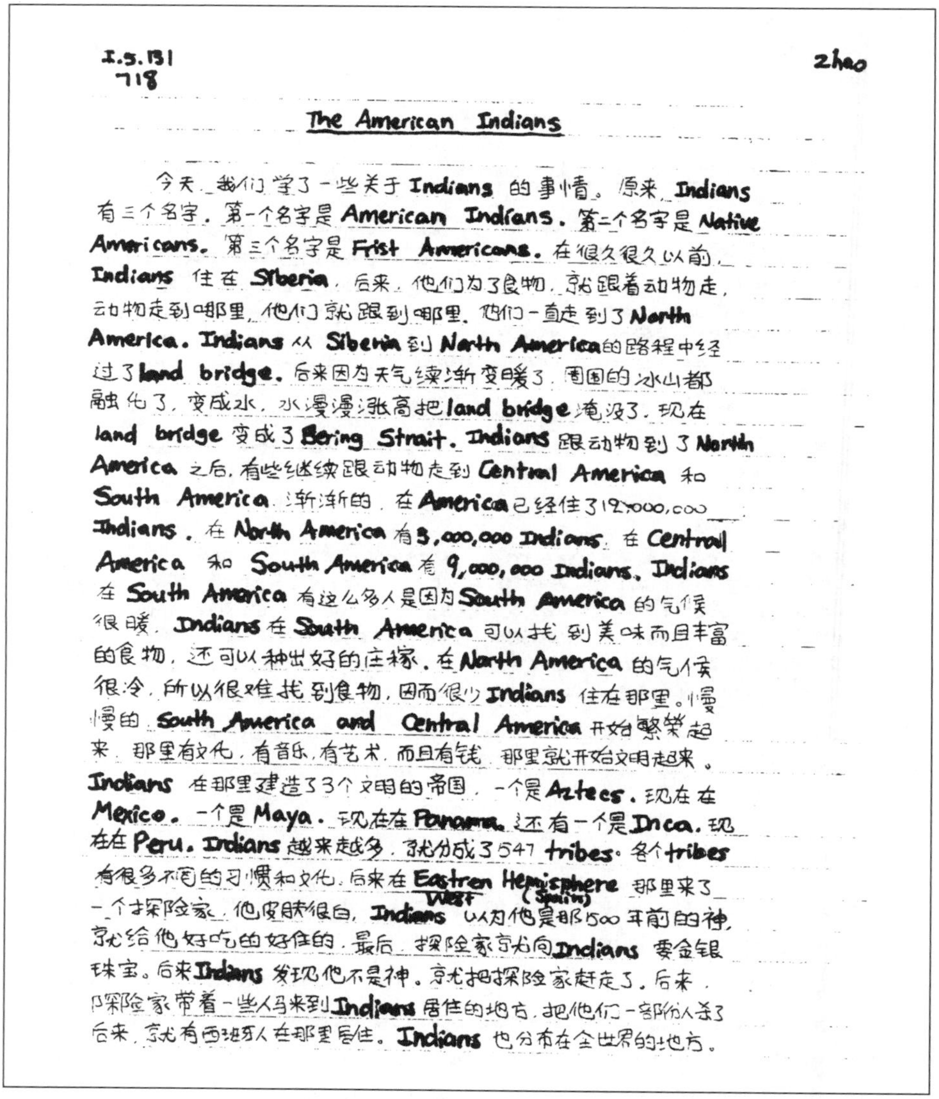

zhao

The American Indians

今天，我们学了一些关于 Indians 的事情。原来 Indians 有三个名字。第一个名字是 American Indians。第二个名字是 Native Americans。第三个名字是 Frist Americans。在很久很久以前，Indians 住在 Siberia。后来，他们为了食物，就跟着动物走，动物走到哪里，他们就跟到哪里。他们一直走到了 North America。Indians 从 Siberia 到 North America 的路程中经过了 land bridge。后来因为天气缘渐变暖了，周围的冰山都融化了，变成水，水漫漫涨高把 land bridge 淹没了。现在 land bridge 变成了 Bering Strait。Indians 跟动物到了 North America 之后，有些继续跟动物走到 Central America 和 South America。渐渐的，在 America 已经住了12,000,000 Indians。在 North America 有3,000,000 Indians。在 Central America 和 South America 有9,000,000 Indians。Indians 在 South America 有这么多人是因为 South America 的气候很暖。Indians 在 South America 可以找到美味而且丰富的食物，还可以种出好的庄稼。在 North America 的气候很冷，所以很难找到食物，因而很少 Indians 住在那里。慢慢的 South America and Central America 开始繁荣起来。那里有文化，有音乐，有艺术，而且有钱。那里就开始文明起来。Indians 在那里建造了3个文明的帝国，一个是 Aztecs。现在在 Mexico。一个是 Maya。现在在 Panama。还有一个是 Inca。现在在 Peru。Indians 越来越多，就分成了547 tribes。各个 tribes 有很多不同的习惯和文化。后来在 Eastren Hemisphere 那里来了一个探险家。他皮肤很白，Indians 以为他是那500年前的神，就给他好吃的好住的。最后，探险家竟尤向 Indians 要金银珠宝。后来 Indians 发现他不是神，竟尤把探险家赶走了。后来，探险家带着一些人马来到 Indians 居住的地方，把他们一部份人杀了。后来，就有西班牙人在那里居住。Indians 也分布在全世界的地方。

Figure 4.15 *A piece dated September 25, written three weeks later, was switched to Chinese-dominant writing mixed with some English words.*

studied, she was certainly more confident in her native language than English. The teacher gave her an "Excellent" for this piece, which indicated that she did a stellar job in presenting what she learned about the topic. Qi claims (1998) that "[t]he higher the general level of knowledge demands a task had, the more language-switching the [ELL] was inclined to use as an explicit or implicit problem-solving strategy in handling the task" (421).

ELLs' recursive moments in their writing development from native language to English suggests that just because ELLs reach a certain fluency in English writing, it doesn't mean they have the same proficiency in all writing they do. As we saw previously, Ming and Jing moved smoothly and orderly in their daily journal writing from their native language to English within a school year. But that doesn't mean they can do the same when they engage in academic writing. As shown by portfolio work, students know the best language form to use to appropriately present their ideas and feelings. When writing daily journals, they use communicative language: everyday vocabulary and oral language expression (sentence structure). Usually, if students write every day, they can attain a certain fluency in daily journal writing (to express their daily activities) within a school year like Jing and Ming did. But once they are required to do academic writing, which is often content specific, they must learn a new language, a new genre, and a new discourse. This is as how we describe ELLs' learning: fluency in the hallway does not necessarily mean proficiency in the classroom. We may come to the realization that in the four stages of ELLs' writing development, ELLs don't move linearly from one to another. They travel back and forth depending on the complexity of the topics they write about as well as the purpose, genre, and intended audience of their writing. Code-switching is a strategy that ELLs will frequently adopt to problem-solve a linguistically demanding task.

When we truly value what students say in their writing, we appreciate their appropriate choices of language use and accept and encourage this freedom. Once our students feel free to choose among language forms to express themselves, they are becoming true writers rather than merely practicing writing for school work. Our students can sense what we expect them to show in their writing. When we value their ideas, they will present them and display their competence as writers.

Assess ELL Writers and Tailor
Instruction to Meet Their Needs

Teachers approach me with questions like: How do I assess the ELLs' progress if they move back and forth among the four stages of the writing development? When do I know they are able to write in English? I tell them that portfolios provide a holistic and accurate way to assess ELLs' writing development. Because different genres and topics may demand different language usage, ELLs may display writing fluency in a certain topic, area, or genre, but not in others.

We haven't done enough to teach ELLs to be real writers. Many teachers still believe that we need to teach them to write correctly first and their native language of ELLs can only be used as a springboard before they can express themselves in proper English. However, while ELLs' work may show that they are able to write "correctly" in certain types of writing, this doesn't necessarily mean they have the same fluency and proficiency in other types of writing. They must choose the language or mixed-language usage that enables them to best express themselves effectively and freely move back and forth between languages to express themselves fully and authentically. Through reading multiple writing samples in students' portfolios we can begin to understand the recursive nature of their writing development.

In teaching ELLs to write, we need to understand the complexity of their composing process, which may be constrained by their limited English proficiency and may reflect the interplay of two or more languages. We need not only welcome their native language into their writing development, but also see it as part of their writing and thinking process. Today we see writers moving back and forth between two languages as they try to express themselves fully. Tomorrow, we may see them skillfully meshing their native language and English to form a unique style of writing identified by bilingual or multilingual writers. What kind of writers (or nonwriters) they will become tomorrow depends on how we help and value them in their writing development today.

Teaching ELLs to Write   ~ 5

This chapter explores writing instruction for ELLs. It first looks at secondary writing instruction in the content areas, and then at elementary writing instruction using a model of collaboration between ESL and regular classroom teachers.[1]

ELLs at the secondary level are required to learn the same requisite subjects as their English-proficient peers. Some schools have bilingual programs where the ELLs can learn certain subjects such as science, social studies, and math in their first language, but many schools don't have any bilingual programs or can't provide bilingual service for all their ELLs. Therefore, some are simply put in regular classrooms, where every day, these students spend between three and five periods learning the same content subjects as their peers. Writing is an essential way for all students to learn content and language, no matter which language they are using to study the subjects. Unfortunately, among the classes I've observed at the secondary school level, the content-area classrooms require the least amount of writing. Many still use workbooks to fill in the blanks or answer questions that require yes-or-no, one-word, or short-phrase responses. ELLs are given textbooks to read that they can barely understand. They go

---

[1]Some content in this chapter was published in a chapter of *Teaching the Neglected "R,"* by Thomas Newkirk and Richard Kent (see Fu 2007b) and as an article in *Changing English* (Fu 2007a).

through the book chapter by chapter and do all exercises required, but learn little. When they use the workbooks or answer questions after the reading, they basically copy words from the text onto the worksheets with very little comprehension.

Studying in content areas not only calls for learning different subjects, but also the academic language pertaining to the subjects and topics covered. As noted earlier, it takes five to seven years to develop academic language proficiency, in contrast to two or three years to develop communicative English—in part because the academic language is more abstract and less tied to familiar context. Yet ELLs at the secondary level don't have five to seven years to wait: they have to move along in content-knowledge learning with their English-proficient peers.

Most content-area teachers at the secondary level don't feel trained to teach language, let alone writing. Unskilled in reaching ELLs, they simply teach the topics and leave the students to memorize facts, rules, or formulas they barely understand yet. In order for ELL students to learn content information and develop academic language, they have to write, which means going beyond answering questions or simply transferring words from textbooks onto worksheets. Writing in connection with learning content knowledge will help ELLs not only understand the subjects they are taught, but also develop academic English proficiency.

Reading for ELLs in Content Areas

Writing successfully in the content areas is closely associated with reading proficiency in the content areas. Most content-area study involves reading textbooks that are written in condensed language and inundated with compact information. ELLs have a hard time digesting it all. In order for them to write about what they study, they need to understand what they are reading first. The dilemma for content-area teachers teaching ELLs in secondary schools is that the textbooks they use are designed for students with English proficiency. In my interviews of thirty high school ELLs, most said they comprehended 30 percent or less of the content covered in their textbooks. Later, their teacher told me that, actually, many could understand no more than 10 percent of the textbook used in his class. When ELLs can hardly understand the text they are assigned to read, it is impossible for them to present their learning in writing.

Richard Allington (2005), a well-known researcher in reading, recommends putting books in the students' hands that they can actually understand. Very few textbooks at the secondary level are easily comprehended by ELLs. As educators, we need to go beyond textbooks and search for picture books written on the same topics in the content areas. For example, there are pictures books, information books, and chapter books on the social studies and science topics covered at the secondary level, such as the Civil War, slavery, historical figures, immigrants, American government, ecosystems, the rain forest, and natural disasters.

Many teachers at the secondary level are not comfortable assigning books seemingly written for elementary-age children. They think that these books do not cover enough of the necessary information, and that to use them somehow puts down students at the secondary level. Even though an individual book may not provide all the facts and information that a textbook does, many of them together can provide a great deal of information—in rich contexts and in communicative language that is easier for ELLs to understand. Moreover, if we let students read different books with the same theme or on the same topic, they can learn a lot from each other through mere discussions and book talks. And while it is also true that when we use the books that our ELLs can understand, we may not cover all the topics that the curriculum demands, we know that what we cover in teaching is never equal to the amount students are learning. Ted Sizer (1991) argues that in education, less can be more. Through rich discussion of what the students read, "we may have 'covered' less, but in the end we will have 'uncovered' more" (Walqui 2006, 178).

When we let all our students read different books rather than using one textbook for the entire class, most don't mind choosing books written at their level. For adolescents, it is truly awkward if the rest of the class reads one hardcover textbook, and a few of them are given easy books to read. Some feel so embarrassed that they prefer not to learn anything by holding the same book as their peers rather than reading a book they can actually understand. They forfeit their learning to preserve their social self-image.

For a class with students from diverse learning, language, and academic backgrounds, using one book for the whole class throughout the year is an ineffective approach to instruction.

Many students are victims of our defective instructional approach. It is we teachers who need to revise our teaching by using multiple books at various language levels so we can successfully deal with issues related to adolescents' self-image and help them all learn effectively. Only when ELLs understand their reading and are able to share and talk about their learning can they write to present their newly learned knowledge in the content areas. Reading, and then talking about reading, should be a prerequisite to their writing in the content areas.

Writing for ELLs in Content Areas

According to Applebee and Langer's recent report, *The State of Writing Instruction in America's Schools*, students at the secondary level do not write much: "Two-thirds of students in Grade 8 are expected to spend an hour or less on writing for homework each week, and 40% of twelfth graders report never or hardly ever being asked to write a paper of 3 pages or more" (2006, 2). For ELLs at the secondary level, writing is required much less frequently than for their English-proficient peers (Harklau and Pinnow 2009).

In addition, writing in content areas in our schools is usually restricted to a few expository pieces such as book or lab report, a summary of a reading, or short essay-type answers to questions. The purpose and opportunity for writing in content areas is also limited: as a checkup of understanding for the topics covered in two or three short essays in a year. For the sake of learning in the content areas and for language development, ELLs have to write much more frequently—informally, formally, and in different formats. Writing in content areas should not be very different from what students do in English or ESL classes, where they are required to write either daily or weekly journals; compose reading response journals where they can make person-to-person, text-to-text, and text-to-world connections; and publish work in different genres about their learning and personal lives.

Daily and weekly journals help ELLs use everyday language to connect their learning in the classroom with their lives: their observations of the environment and their community; their views and opinions on the current events locally, nationally, and internationally; and their response to global-warming issues. This kind of free and personal writing related to topics they examine in class will not only connect their academic learning with their personal lives or experiences, but also help them learn more deeply and enhance their cognitive language development.

A reading response journal is a more poignant example of writing than simple answer to questions or marks on a worksheet. The former requires students to use a composing process to organize information in their minds and to find personal words to express their knowledge. The latter require factual recall and repetition of words and concepts created by others.

In the reading response shown in Figure 5.1, a seventh-grade ELL demonstrated his understanding of a Spanish explorer he had studied and his skill of presentation in writing. The reading response also gives students the freedom to decide what they want to present and how they want to present it. When students read different types of books written in different genres on different topics in the content areas, they should be guided to try a variety of writing genres to present their learning in those diverse ways. In four New York City middle schools where I worked, ELLs wrote personal narrative, fiction stories, compare/contrast essays, plays, and poetry to present their learning and inquiries and do research in their social studies and science classes. They published their nonfiction books or writing in different genres in magazine formats for scientific topics and put on plays about social studies topics. Their publications demonstrated a solid and broad knowledge, gained through research, of the topics they were studying. They also showed the development of academic English language proficiency (Fu 2003). Their final publications had gone through multiple drafts, revisions, and layers of editing, and were the result of weeks of research that included book reading, Internet searching, note taking on field trips, and personal interviews. Most of these published works were the products of two or three students collaborating on one topic according to their interests.

Spain Explorer 1.

    today I in S.S. class learn in
Spain have a Explorer he name is
Vasco Nunez de Balboa, Balboa he first
go to Hispaniola, the Hispaniola final
become two place, first is Haiti
海上也, seacond is Dominican Republie
致明足地, then Balboa dnot think in
hispaniola this place, he want to 别
的 place, Balboa 躲 in 一舟船上, this
船的 of captain 对水手 very bad, Balboa
出来 and 水手把 captain 邦进海里, he
oneself do of captain, they 经过了
many swaps and many jungles, they
arrived panama, then panama be
they 钱光了. they 互近见 Indina, Indina
tell they if 你们 need to go find 金银
珠宝 need 往西走, they start south
America, then they 发现一丁 sea, Balboa help

Figure 5.1   *A Student's Reading Response on Social Study Topic*

Assessing Students' Writing in the Content Areas

Asking students to write more increases the workload for the teachers. But if less work for us means less or no learning for students, we have no right to take a more laissez-faire approach in teaching. But it doesn't mean we should make our work unreasonably overwhelming and unmanageable. Usually the teachers in the content areas at the secondary level have 120 to 150 students. It is hard to read or grade all the students' writing when pieces are so numerous and in different formats. Reading ELLs' writing is hard because each piece is packed with errors and nonidiomatic expressions (see Figure 5.1). Content-area teachers can get so frustrated at reading their students' work that they may just let them write less, offer multiple-choice exercises, or simply go back to easy-to-grade worksheets requiring one- or two-word answers.

We don't have to read each piece of our students' work. But that doesn't mean we let students write and never attend to it. For daily or weekly journals, we can let students share their writing in groups. This prepares students to talk in groups and have something to say, which connects their learning with their lives. The teacher can go around and join the conversation from group to group, randomly checking the students' work. We can do the same with their reading response journals. We can put the students who read the same book or different books into book talk groups. Their reading response journals prepare their book talk, which demonstrates reading comprehension. The teacher can sit in on the discussions, one group at a time, listening to the students' book share just like their peers without reading their work beforehand. For ELLs, this kind of talk is very beneficial to their learning and language development. For daily or weekly journals or reading responses, I recommend not reading each piece or paying excessive attention to how it is written. This beginning writing can be like people speaking to themselves and will improve gradually over time and with intensive language contact. I may check it to see whether students do the writing or how long they write, but that is the extent of it. The opportunities for them to share in groups based on this writing should give them enough incentive to continue, and enough time to improve their work gradually. Kohn points out, "Homework in the best classrooms is not checked—it is shared" (2006, 37).

Writing for publication takes time and involves not only content learning, but also reading, research skills, writing, and language development. Sometimes, many topics under one big theme are studied as a unit, such as countries and cultures across the world. Different groups read and research different aspects of the theme, and individual students in each group take a particular focus for in-depth research and draft their individual work to fit in the collaborative product. Teachers give directions and lessons on general issues and skills and facilitate the group work through minilessons, group and individual conferences, and class demonstrations.

Usually the teachers at Dr. Sun Yat Sen Middle School do two or three long-term projects of this kind in a year. If we give students enough time, if we let them work with each other on their research and help one another with their writing, if we only periodically or selectively read their work, it should be manageable. Since our students are at different levels with their English ability, we should also accept their work while holding different expectations for individual abilities. Some can write longer, some shorter; some can write to discuss more complicated issues, and some can present simple facts, as long as they put forth their best effort.

That said, the errors in ELLs' writing can sometimes be overwhelming, especially to content-area teachers not used to reading writing with errors and strange expressions and include ungrammatical sentence structures, spelling mistakes, improper word choices, and nonidiomatic expressions. The overwhelming number of errors can block our minds from reading on or even trying to understand what the students are writing. In working with ELLs, we do need to learn to read through that "broken" surface structure (Fu 2003). Otherwise, it will be impossible to focus on the idea or content of their writing when we read their beginning drafts. It is like listening to a person with limited English proficiency; if we don't try hard to understand what he tries to say, but focus on correcting how he speaks, the speaker will stop speaking or communicating with us completely. If we give our attention to errors in ELLs' writing during the draft stage, students will focus their attention on producing correct English, which would turn writing into language practice rather than writing for content presentation and self-expression.

This doesn't mean we should ignore all surface errors. I interviewed an ESL teacher after I saw a final copy of one of his beginning ELL's work, which was corrected from the first draft but still contained many grammatical errors (see Figure 5.2a and 5.2b). Here is his explanation:

> When I work with my beginning ELLs, I pay much attention to what they try to say, and I help them to get the meaning across. When I help students edit their work, I don't help them correct all the errors, which would require me to rewrite every sentence for them, but only enough to be understood.
>
> For this student [Zhang], this was the first piece he ever completed in English, and it took him quite a long time to finish this piece. . . . I want him to continue to write and take risks on his own.

Seeing the difference between the draft and the final typed copy, I understand what this teacher meant by not correcting all the errors. We propose in our writing instruction to teach writers rather than simply teaching writing. This teacher certainly holds this view in his teaching practice.

By working through many drafts and sharing their work repeatedly with their peers, many ELLs should have made their work better understood with fewer errors than the beginning draft. Editing can take a lot of time, and is a good opportunity for ELLs to work on their English skills. I recommend that we let students help each other edit their work as much as possible and continue their editing work in the ESL room, which is contextualized language learning. Just like improving English speaking, by writing frequently the students will improve their writing and language skills from one piece to another. Making every piece perfect doesn't always produce good writers, but may instead inhibit students from taking risks in learning.

I also suggest that content-area teachers work closely with the ESL resource room teachers. Let ELLs continue their writing in their ESL rooms or have their ESL teachers help them with revision and editing. This would not only reduce the content-area teacher's work considerably, but

Figure 5.2a *The First Draft of Zhang's Story*

also connect the learning between ESL and subject classrooms. ESL teachers can assist ELLs with revising and editing their work and help them finalize their products. The following is a collaborative model for ESL and regular classrooms teachers in an elementary school that can help ELLs become writers in English. Ideally, teachers at the secondary level can gain some insights from the practice of elementary school teachers.

My first time

    My first time see look like dog big mouse run for street I and my father was very shocked.
    Its teeth are 3 inches long, Its tail are 20 inches long, Its 4 leges are 5 inches long. Its eyes are red color and one people run for this mouse. My father walk for this people talk this people and I run to this people listen my father say, "This big mouse one day eat who many food."

This people say, "This mouse one day eat 15 pound for food." My father say, "This big mouse 1 hours run who long." This people say, "This mouse 1 hours run 80 miles look like a car the miles." I say, "This mouse live in where." This people say, "This live in dog house." I and my father to this people talk so long.
    This people go home. I and my father walk to home, I say, "My first time see this this big mouse."

Figure 5.2b   *The Final Draft of Zhang's Story*

A Collaboration Model for ESL and Regular Classroom Teachers

The collaborative work presented here took place in a Chinatown elementary school and demonstrates how two teachers worked together to solve their teaching dilemma and help their ELLs improve their writing and language learning as effectively as possible. The teaching dilemma these two teachers faced represents a prevalent situation in U.S. schools. According to New York State law, ELL students who haven't passed the mandatory LAB test (Language Assessment Battery) need to be provided with 180 to 360 minutes of ESL service weekly. Usually, one or two ESL teachers have to serve seventy to eighty or more students (about 20 percent of the student population). They see students in every grade level for one or two periods a day in classes that may be scattered all over the building. In the mainstream classrooms, these students are struggling to learn the same curriculum as their English-proficient peers. "Chasing the wind" is a metaphor often used to describe ELL students in this kind of situation, where they don't seem to be getting anywhere, but are exhausted from the futile chase (Hruska 2000).

Both classroom and ESL teachers sense their ELLs' frustration in struggling to understand what goes on in their classrooms. Regular classroom teachers wish that ESL teachers would move students faster to develop their English language ability because the students don't know how to begin to handle their reading and writing work. On the flip side, ESL teachers wish that the classroom teacher would adjust the curriculums for ELLs and give them more individual attention. ESL teachers feel that since ELLs spend five or six hours a day in the regular classroom, they should get more out of being there than they could in the one or two periods a day spent in the ESL program. In addition, the classroom teachers think that ESL teachers only teach the basics of language, but not much about literacy content such as reading and writing. Conversely, ESL teachers feel that the classroom teachers don't know how to help ELL students develop the skills and vocabulary they need, and the reading or writing contents they teach are simply beyond what the ELL students are capable of. This situation, in which each side wants the other to do more than their fair share for ELLs, has caused tension between ESL and classroom teachers in many schools (Penfield 1987; Roessingh 2004; Schnorr and Davern 2005).

In addition, there is usually a missing link between the ESL and regular classroom curriculums. This disconnection makes the students feel lost when they return to their mainstream classroom community after being away for one or two periods. They are usually behind anyway and can't follow the instruction in the regular classroom. And they feel even more out of place when they come back to the classroom after their work with the ESL teacher; they don't know what is going on and can't participate in class activities. It is like entering the stage in the middle of a show. Therefore, they tend to either flounder or give up and chat among themselves. In order for them to join class activities or feel part of the class, the teacher has to reteach what she has just taught to the whole class. Being in this kind of situation every day is troubling for both ELLs and the classroom teachers (Penfield 1987; Hruska 2000; Roessingh 2004).

To solve this problem, many schools adopt a push-in model, which means that instead of taking ELLs out, the ESL teacher comes into the classroom to serve the students. Theoretically, the ESL teacher would try to help ELLs do what the rest of the class is doing, which means helping them fit into the mainstream curriculum (New 1993). This may sound ideal, but other problems arise. First, there are not enough ESL teachers to do push-ins, one room at a time. Second, the ESL teachers feel they have their own instructional agenda for the individual students. Third, it is impossible for them to know the curriculum of every teacher in every grade. For these major reasons, the push-in model rarely fills its intended role, and is used only when an ESL teacher has a free spot to fill with one or two students. Very often, the ESL teachers work with ELLs in the corner of the classroom with their own lesson plans, which may have little to do with the regular classroom's curriculum. The push-in model is basically an ESL service in a mainstream setting rather than special help that assists ELLs fitting into the classroom learning. A better recommendation to solve the disconnection in ELLs' learning situation might be a collaboration between ESL and regular classroom teachers.

PS 126, an elementary school in lower Manhattan of New York City, had a successful model of collaboration in literacy instruction for ELLs between their pull-out/push-in ESL teacher and the regular teacher. In this school, the newly arrived immigrant children made up 20 percent of the student population, and most came from families who could give little support for school work. With 1.5 ESL support positions available, the school could only afford a pull-out or push-in ESL program, and all ELL students were placed in the regular classrooms from day one of their arrival at the school. The administrators at the school fully understood the challenges for both teachers and students, and were trying hard to make the best of the existing situation. They had frequent faculty meetings in the morning or at lunchtime to discuss the problems and help teachers work on finding solutions. "How the ESL and classroom teachers should work together to enhance the development of ELL students' literacy and English language skills" was the theme proposed to the faculty at one such meeting. Amy, an ESL teacher, and, Renee, a fourth-grade classroom teacher, took the challenge and experimented in a yearlong collaboration.

Amy Huang had been an ESL teacher in PS 126 for two years. She was young and energetic, arriving at school an hour early and staying late after school every day to give ELL students extra help. She served about thirty ELLs of varying levels each day using pull-out or push-in combined models. Though she could see obvious improvement with her ELLs' English language development month by month, she was frustrated because she felt that her ELLs didn't do much in the regular classrooms. With most of the day spent in the regular classrooms, students should have read and written more there than with her, or at least practiced or used what they learned in her room with their classroom work. She wished she were able to work with her ELLs more, but it was impossible.

Renee Houser had been a fourth-grade teacher in PS 126 for three years. She loved teaching and her kids. She was not afraid to try anything that might lead to her students' learning improvement. She had twenty students, five of whom were ELL students and whose LAB test scores showed that they had very limited English proficiency and needed ESL support daily. Renee had different lesson plans for these students and tried various ways to reach them: working with them in small groups, conferring individually with them on their writing, and pairing them with the more English-proficient students who also spoke their native language. But with so many students to attend to, Renee couldn't give her ELL students the time each day that she desired. She noticed while she was teaching the whole class or working with other students that her ELLs looked either confused or lost. She knew if they could be engaged in learning all the time, they could have made greater progress than they had.

Collaboration is time-consuming, especially for teachers whose days are already packed with too much extraneous work. In addition, both Amy and Renee were still working on their master's degrees. They didn't have much spare time. They had to do their collaboration during lunch or prep time, or during an hour or two before and after school. Renee paints a brief picture of how these two teachers collaborated:

> Amy and I met briefly in the morning as we both arrived early, just to check and make sure our schedule worked, etc. This was nice for several reasons: we could update one another on kids' progress. Sometimes we saw different things, depending on different environments; some kids were more vocal with her in a small group. Amy would also attend our weekly grade level meetings where we sat and planned and problem solved . . . Often Amy and I would sit down and compare our notes about the students. Amy spent a lot of time observing my teaching style and content in reading and writing, so that she could then build on the concepts. Amy and I could brainstorm together ideas for the entire class, and how to help ELL students.
>
> Toward the middle and end of the year, Amy would commit an hour of her time to be in my class during the minilesson and then was able to form a small group and/or work with individual students in writing. . . . Sometimes we even worked together to co-teach a small group. This was AWESOME!!! The kids' writing improved a lot with our collaboration.

Collaboration on a Nonfiction Writing Unit

Amy and Renee's collaboration on a nonfiction writing unit demonstrates specifically how they worked together to help their ELLs grow as writers, which can be summarized as planning their curriculum, observing each other's teaching, coteaching and assessing their students, and setting goals for individual students together. Writing and reading workshops were conducted every day in Renee's room, and she taught a variety of genres through connected instruction of reading and writing. Chart 5.3 illustrates in detail how Renee and Amy aligned their instruction in both classroom settings with ELL students in a nonfiction unit, which lasted eight weeks and focused on feature article writing. Before the unit started, Renee and Amy spent many hours before winter break planning how they could connect their instruction in both settings and help ELL students develop their specific understanding and writing of a feature article.

Working in both classroom settings for eight weeks and through a dozen drafts, all five ELL students published their feature articles along

Dates	Regular Instruction in the Classroom (Renee)	ESL Push-in and Small Group for ELLs (Renee and/or Amy)	ESL Pull-out to ESL Room (Amy)
Jan. 6–9	Reading and discussing nonfiction and learning about feature article	Small-group instruction on the elements of nonfiction and feature article	Reading nonfiction, discussing nonfiction elements and feature article writing
Jan. 13–14	Choose topics for writing	Individual conference with ELLs	Work on topic choice
Jan. 15–16	First draft: quick writing of what is on your mind	Help individual students stay on track	Continue to work on the first draft
Jan. 17	Reread the first draft and work on organization	Work with ELLs on how to group ideas into themes	Continue to work on their writing
Jan. 20–21	How to do interviews and get data through interviews	Small-group instruction on interview questions	Learn how to ask questions and take notes
Jan. 22–23	Conduct interviews	Practice interviews	Put notes into sentences
Jan. 24	How to report the interview data	Go over their interview notes	Organize interview information
Jan. 27–28	Work on the second draft with interview data	Confer with ELLs for their writing	Continue their writing: learn the vocabulary and sentence structure needed for writing
Jan. 29–30	What is second-hand data?	Help ELLs find out what second-hand information they need for their work	Search for books and on Internet for second-hand data
Feb. 2–5	Research second-hand data through reading	Reading and conferring with ELLs	Continue to read for second-hand data
Feb. 9–12	Add the research data into the writing	Take notes of second-hand data	Weave second-hand data into writing

Chart 5.3   *Renee and Amy's Collaborative Instruction for ELLs on a Nonfiction Unit*

Dates	Regular Instruction in the Classroom (Renee)	ESL Push-in and Small Group for ELLs (Renee and/or Amy)	ESL Pull-out to ESL Room (Amy)
Feb. 16–18	Work on revision	Confer with ELLs on how to use direct quotes	Continue to work on their writing
Feb. 19–28	Revision and editing, polish and publishing	Work on revision cut/paste Minilesson on quotation marks	Learn skills: verb tenses, spelling, and sentence structure, punctuation and paragraphing Publishing Help ELLs practice reading their work and present to the class

Chart 5.3   *(Continued)*

with their peers. Their final work was typed with digital illustrations, read aloud to the class, and posted on the wall together with their peers' work. Seeing them so involved with all the writing activities, Amy and Renee could tell these ELL students had never felt so proud of their work and so connected with their regular classroom peers. After the unit on feature article writing, the class worked on personal narrative, fictional stories, and book reviews. During those lesson units, ELL students received similar support in both settings and went through a similar process: much reading and many drafts of revisions and editing, as shown in the chart. Renee and Amy stated that their ELL students had never completed and published so much writing with such quality, and in the past, fewer ELL students showed as much progress within one year.

Xuhua's Growth as a Writer

Xuhua came to PS 126 immediately after coming to this country. In PS 126 as a new fourth-grade ELL, he had Amy as his ESL teacher and Renee as his regular classroom teacher. Thanks to Amy and Renee's collaboration, Xuhua benefited greatly in his growth as a writer during his first year of study here. Xuhua was a good writer in his native language but had to start with learning the basic English alphabet when he started school in PS 126. He wrote every day in the ESL class and participated in the reading and writing workshops in his regular classroom. Figure 5.4 shows an example of his early writing in the ESL room.

This piece was about snowing. It was the first time he saw snow and he wrote how white soft snowflakes were floating and flying everywhere. One of his peers commented on his writing (see the square in the right corner) and the English words *school*, *sky*, *snow*, *rain*, and *sneeze* were given by the teacher as the key English vocabulary he should learn after writing this piece.

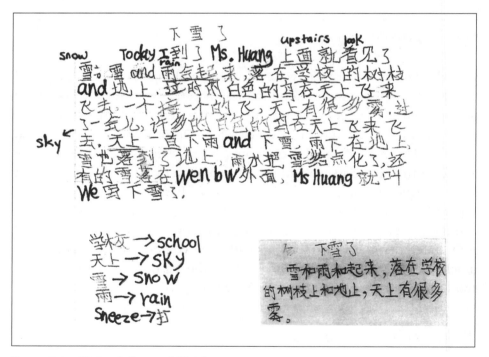

Figure 5.4 *Xuhua's Journal Writing*

His first published picture-pattern book was a counting book:

I see one M & M.
I see two M & M.
I see three M & M.
. . .
I see ten M & M.

He said he wrote this book for young children to learn to count and was proud of his English publication.

In his regular classroom, he wrote during the writing workshop time. From September to January, he completed several fictional stories in Chinese, entitled "Three pigs build their houses," "A toothless tiger," "A little pig and a wolf who likes to fart," and "A gold and silver flower girl and a black bear." He shared his writing with four other ELLs, and enjoyed their elated responses to his work. He said he read a lot of stories like this in Chinese and loved to write animal stories, and he relished the fiction genre. After Christmas, he started to write his stories in English. In March, he published his first story written in English as this:

King
Long time ago, a lion in the woods, animals told lion do this wood king. One day, lion going to the woods and said, "get me the food." Then everybody go home took his food, a monkey came, he took a banana, and cat took a fish. When everyone cook his food, and lion was very happy, because he is the king. He ask animals do what, everybody go to do what.
   One day, a tiger come and lion said, "What are you doing baby." And tiger was very angry, then he push the lion, and lion tell everybody to fight the tiger, then the tiger went to ran, and the king fight the tiger's eye's, and the tiger ran away and the lion was so happy.

Xuhua continued to write his favorite stories and managed to publish another one in May entitled "Why the cat scared to the dog because. . . ." In the writing workshops, Xuhua wrote stories, and in the reading workshops, Xuhua was required to write reading responses. He said he didn't enjoy writing reading responses as much as writing fiction stories, because

"I could write anything I wanted. I could imagine, make up anything. It was much fun writing fictions." In the end, he did learn to write reading responses comparable to his peers. By April, his reading responses were written entirely in English. The following is a book review he wrote in May:

> I have the book. This is the place for me, by Joanna Cole, it was funny story. Why it was a funny story because Morty the bear was always breaking things in his house, he was so big, he couldn't help it. He broke his chair, his table, his door and his anything, but he did not fix his anything. He found a new house, but it had a dragon, and it was too small, and it was too thin and it could sink, and it was scary. So he came back to his old house to fix the door, window, table, and chair, now the old house was as good as new, and Marty say, "This is the place for me, it is much better than my old house." Morty was happy to came to his old house to fix anything, and his house was new.

Even though his writing still contained many errors, and was very much at the inter-language stage, he was comfortable writing in English. As a shy boy, he preferred writing in English than speaking in English. When he wanted to have one of the ELLs as his reading partner, he wrote a request to Renee:

> Dear Ms. Houser
> I wan Lin Ge do my partner:
>
> 1. Lin Ge is good.
> 2. I can work Lin Ge do homework.
> 3. I with Lin Ge is good friend.

And Renee responded him also in writing:

> Dear Xuhua,
> These are some important reasons to think about when you pick a reading partner. How will you pick your books? Let me know your thoughts.
>
> Good luck,
>
> Ms Houser

With Amy and Renee's help and encouragement, by late spring, Xuhua was able to do all his writing in English in both the regular classroom and the ESL room. Seeing Xuhua's confidence in English writing in May, Amy and Renee decided that it was time to expand Xuhua's writing territory from fiction story writing to a memoir, a genre popular among his peers in the fourth grade. With both Renee and Amy's guidance, Xuhua chose to write his memoir on "Learning to Ride a Bike." He did his first draft on this topic on May 19. For several weeks, Renee worked with him on adding dialogue and details to better illustrate his emotions, and shifting paragraphs to make his writing more organized. When it was ESL time, Amy worked with him on his diction, tense agreement, sentence structures, and transitions between paragraphs. Xuhua worked on this piece in both ESL and regular classrooms for three weeks, from May 19 to June 12, and had nine drafts before he finalized this piece. Here is the beginning of his narrative.

Learn to ride a bike
By Xuhua
My bike is in China. My mother went to the bicycle store to buy a bike for me, but I was not happy about getting a bike, because I didn't know how to ride a bike. First, I needed to learn to how to ride a bike, and I wanted my sister to teach me and help me to learn to ride the bike.

Sometimes, my sister was not there to help me and teach me, so I rode the bike by myself. I felt scared, and I fell down. I felt angry when I fell down. I hurt my knees, legs and arms, bled and bruise, I was crying. My mother took me to the doctor, my mother said, "Don't ride the bike, because you will get hurt." I answered, "Okay." But I was not happy, my face was sad, because I had fun riding my bike, and I couldn't learn to ride bike. When my mother was not home, I was happy. I was jump on the bed, because I was able to practice riding my bike. Then I wanted to call my friend to go ride the bike with me.

When Xuhua read his piece to the class, his peers cheered for him. They knew how much effort he put into writing this piece. Xuhua was very proud of his accomplishment as well and was especially excited to read the responses his peers wrote on the response sheet. He took the sheet to read in the ESL room and spent the whole class period reading his peers' responses to his memoir, one by one, word by word, with a constant smile on his face (see Figure 5.5).

Xuhau came to Renee and Amy as a good fiction story writer in his native language but had very limited English proficiency. After one year of studying with Renee and Amy, he was able to write in English in multiple genres. He began the year writing in his native language and then

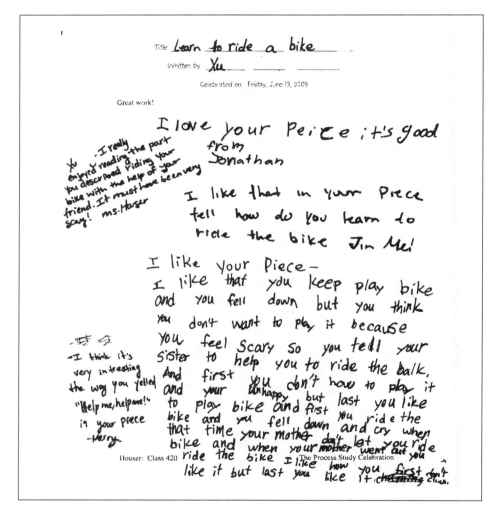

Title: Learn to ride a bike
Written by Xu

Celebrated on: Friday, June 13, 2003

Great work!

Xu - I really enjoyed reading the part you described riding your bike with the help of your friend. It must have been very scary! ms. Houser

I love your Peice; it's good
from
Jonathan

I like that in your Piece
tell how do you learn to
ride the bike Jin Mei!

I like your Piece—
I like that you keep play bike
and you fell down but you think
you don't want to play it because
you feel scary so you tell your
-I think it's sister to help you to ride the balk,
very intresting And first you don't how to play it
the way you yelled and your unhappy but last you like
"Help me, help me!" to play bike and fist you ride the
in your piece bike and you fell down and cry when
-Henry. that time your mother don't let you ride
bike and when your mother went out you
Houser: Class 420 ride the bike I like The Process Study Celebration
like it but last you like it cheating class.

Figure 5.5   *Peer-Response Sheet to Xuhau's Story*

transitioned to mixed-language writing. And from March to June, the end of the school year, he published many pieces entirely in English. There were three fiction stories, one memoir, one feature article, and three book reviews. Just like learning to ride his bike, Xuhua had ups and downs in learning to write in English throughout the year, but he was persistent. With Renee and Amy's collaborative scaffolding in both regular and ESL classrooms and with his peers' influence and support, Xuhua developed from a good story writer in his native language to a writer in English of multiple genres.

Conclusion

ELLs will achieve obvious growth as writers if they are guided to write in all subject areas they are studying and have continuity in their study in various programs and classrooms. Teachers need to work together to help ELLs develop as writers as well as language learners. Thus, I emphasize that we should:

◆ Provide plenty of writing opportunities.

◆ Teach writing across content-subject areas.

◆ Understand and guide students through writing stages.

◆ Give students the freedom in their language choice for expression.

◆ Allow students to move back and forth from their native writing to English writing.

◆ Urge bilingual, ESL, and regular classroom teachers to collaborate on their curriculum for ELLs' literacy and language development.

Writing is the most challenging skill for ELLs, and, as stated before, it is often the least emphasized. From elementary to graduate school, I hear frequent complaints from instructors that their ELLs just can't write. But we rarely ask if they have ever been taught to write, or how they have been taught to write, or if they have had any teachers in their schooling who have helped them express what they wanted to articulate in English through writing. We must take more time and make a greater effort in teaching writing to English language learners. If we do, our students will grow as writers and achieve their language proficiency.

Language Instruction Through Writing

6

This chapter focuses on language instruction for ELLs through writing. Specifically, it addresses how to using writing to teach ELLs speaking, reading, and other language skills such as grammar, spelling, and vocabulary. English proficiency is a necessity for all ELLs, and the most effective language instruction helps them develop their language skills in the context of meaningful reading/writing and through authentic communication. Writing incorporates all language skills—grammar, vocabulary, spelling, word choice, and oral language communication. ELLs can develop this language proficiency through writing—by practicing and reinforcing the language skills they are learning.

Developing Speaking Skills Through Writing

Language is for communication. ELLs need to develop their oral English proficiency in order to participate in everyday school and community activities. Children learn their native tongue in a natural environment where they are immersed in the language and learn it through frequent and intimate interactions with the people around them. In contrast, ELLs learn English mostly in academic settings, and have fewer opportunities to practice speaking English outside of schools. But first- and second-language acquisition share similar processes (see Chart 6.1) that parallel in some ways the four writing stages that ELLs go through.

The oral language development stages for ELLs are comparable to the four stages of writing development, though they may not spontaneously take place in ELLs' language acquisition. During the silent stage, ELLs communicate with others in their first language. When they develop some English language skills, they start to utter a few English words to respond to others or in class (telegraphic stage). This parallels to the code-switching stage in ELLs' writing transition. During this stage, ELLs may insert English words into their native language speaking. In both oral and writing development, ELLs will go through an inter-language stage (also defined as the intermediate stage) before they reach the advanced proficiency stage.

Speaking is an interactive skill; writing is more solitary. Interacting with others requires other skills, such as courage, risk taking, understanding of accepted cultural and social behaviors, and emotional security. Speaking is the most challenging to ELLs, especially for those who came to this country at an older age, because it requires speakers to quickly organize thoughts, make meaningful points, choose the right words, and speak with

Stages	L1 Acquisition	L2 Acquisition	ELL Writing Transitions
Preproduction	Listening stage	Silent stage	Native writing
Emergent	Telegraphic stage (use key words in expression)	Telegraphic stage (use one or two words or short phrases in expression)	Code-switching
Beginning production (intermediate)	Begin applying rules	Inter-language stage	Inter-language stage
Advanced	Close to adult language	Close to conventional English	Close to conventional English

Chart 6.1   *Parallel of L1 Acquisition, L2 Learning, and ELLs' Writing Transitions*

proper pronunciation spontaneously. I found that ELLs in the upper elementary and secondary schools began to write in English sooner (code-switching and inter-language stages) than they were willing to speak up in English. If we expect ELLs to participate in class discussion or group sharing, we need to give them time to rehearse their speaking out, even for a small-group share or read-aloud. This rehearsal activity will shorten their silent period and enable them to participate sooner in the class discussion.

John Lo, a sixth-grade ESL teacher at Dr. Sun Yat Sen Middle School, used weekly journal writing systematically to help his students develop their speaking ability, which, he agreed, was the most challenging for his ELLs:

> They simply refused to speak in class. When I asked them questions, they either nodded or shook their heads or gave me one word "yes or no" response. It was like pulling teeth to get them say a few words in English, even I required them to repeat the words from the book. So I decided to put effort in helping them to speak up.

John requires his students to write in their journals twice a week to describe their daily experiences. When he noticed that the students' journals contained listlike entries, he assigned general topics, such as describing your favorite hometown food or a place you like to visit. John would work with each student weekly to prepare them to share their journals with the class. His students' writing ranged from writing in Chinese to code-switching and inter-language writing. He would help students who wrote their journals in Chinese to translate a few key sentences to English. If students used code-switching and inter-language writing, he would help them smooth a little bit of their writing. Then he would help all the students practice reading their writing fluently before they read to the class. He pushed his students from reading their work to the class to speaking to the class without reading their words. He had them record their speaking on a tape recorder and let them practice on their own until they reached certain fluency. About using journals to help his students learn to speak English, he said:

> I pushed everything orally. What is the point of having them write their life experiences, just for me to read? I want them to be able to express, to talk about, and tell others about their lives. I want them to express their meaning

first—grammar is not a big deal at the beginning stage—and we will deal with grammar later. Just like letting them write any language in their journals, I let them use any ways to express themselves orally—broken English, English with a few Chinese characters—as long as they tell us about their lives. I want them not to be afraid to speak out, especially in English. At this stage, I help them to write, to speak, to use their writing to speak, to read aloud, to practice using English in public. Our class is their public place, since there is no place in Chinatown they can practice their English speaking. It is hard for them at first, but they struggle, they do it. Now they want to do it. (quoted in Fu 2003, 51)

At this point, John's purpose was to help his ELLs speak up and learn to talk about their life experiences in English rather than helping them speak English correctly. When these students listened to each other read and talked about their lives, they could identify with each other's interests and life experiences. It was easier for them to listen to their peers read and share than listening to their teacher's read-aloud. In addition, by listening to their peers' writing, they learned to improve their own writing. Writing helps ELLs speak better, which, in turn, helps them write better, because we tend to write as we speak.

At the beginning stage of oral language development, teachers should do just as John did with his students: use writing to prepare them to speak up. Don't pay too much attention to grammar or pronunciation as long as they can be understood. Accents may always exist in ELLs' English speech, particular for those who came to this country after their elementary school education. Since we all speak with a certain accent, we should not be too concerned with ELLs' accent, but accept their speech and put our efforts into helping them speak up, express what they want to say, and speak clearly and idiomatically.

Our classrooms may be the only place where ELLs can get help with their oral language development, because most don't live in English-speaking environments. Thirty to sixty percent of ELLs reside in the non-English-speaking communities and go to school with peers who speak their ethnic languages (Ruiz-de-Velasco and Fix 2000), especially in metropolitan areas like New York's Chinatown and East Harlem (which is Spanish dominant). They don't have much opportunity outside of their classrooms to speak English or communicate with proficient English speakers, let alone give a lengthy speech in English. As John put it, "Our class is their public place, since there is no place [outside of their classrooms] they can practice their English speaking." Writing to assist ELLs' oral language presentation enables them to speak up with more confidence.

Teaching Reading Through Writing

An excellent strategy for helping struggling readers improve their oral reading fluency is to have them read their own writing because the content is familiar to them and the language is at their comprehensive level. This strategy would benefit ELLs in the same way. We should systematically use ELLs' writing to help them develop their reading skills. When they write in their native language, we can ask other students who speak their language to translate the main idea of their writing, and then let the translation becomes a reading text for them. There are translation software programs that can translate one language to another. Students type their writing into the computer and the program translates the writing into English. Though the translation may not be as precise as the original text, it is good enough to present the main ideas of their work. All ELLs' published work can be used for oral reading fluency practice, after it has been through many drafts and editing, and then the students can share their work with the class.

Selina, another ESL teacher at Dr. San Yat Sen Middle School, used wordless picture books to help her ELLs write in English. Students produced different versions of one wordless picture book, and Selina conferred with each of them to revise and edit their work. Students not only practiced reading their own story versions, but also loved to read their peers' papers. The activity of reading each other's version of the same story spurred students to change their writing to be different from the others', so they had to work very hard to be creative and unique as they wrote. When the work was done, they couldn't wait to read each other's creations. Some wordless picture books to use as examples are: *Window* by Jeannie Baker, *Anno's Flea Market* by Mitsumasa Anno, *The Gift* by John Prater, and *The Invitation* by Gabriel Lisowski. Selina maintained that these wordless picture books presented sophisticated concepts that were age appropriate for her early adolescent ELLs. Letting students create their own stories for the book is a great exercise because, in Selina's words:

> Students can write at their own level. Some write a lot for [a] one page picture, some only write one or two sentences based on their English proficiency. By the end, some stories can be very different from the others. The students loved to read each other's stories. The better English proficient students helped the less proficient ones read their stories, and they grew as readers and writers together.

For beginning ELLs at the secondary level, it is hard to find books written in English that are age appropriate and written in a language they can understand. Using wordless picture books for writing and later for reading is a great way to solve this dilemma when teaching upper-grade beginning ELLs to read.

Language Development Through Pattern Book Writing

Pattern books are written with certain language patterns. The language in pattern books is repetitive and predictable, with one or two sentence patterns on one topic throughout a book. "Brown Bear, Brown Bear, what do you see? I see a giraffe (a monkey, a tiger) looking at me," is a typical pattern book. With a one-word (here a different noun for an animal) change, students can create multiple sentences—or a different pattern, such as "Mom, Mom, What do you see? I see a little baby smiling at me." Reading and listening to these kinds of books, ELLs learn certain sentence patterns and vocabulary. By creating their own pattern books, they not only practice the language skills they have learned but begin to use new language to express themselves. For instance, look at this pattern book written by a student and modeled after a pattern book she read:

My teachers
My teacher teaches me to speak English.
My teacher teaches me to count.
My teacher teaches me to draw.
My teacher teaches me to sing and dance.

My teacher teaches me to understand science.
My teacher teaches me to be nice.
I love my teachers.

This simple book contains a lot of grammar concepts: noun and verb agreement, verb tense, inflection ending, possessive adjective, subject and object pronouns, plural forms, infinitive verb, and capitalization. Before recognizing these grammar rules, students gain language experience by reading and writing pattern books. Pattern book series move from one-sentence patterns in one book to multiple-sentence patterns in another. Most pattern books use everyday communicative language. By reading books like this, students develop their language skills and vocabulary, and by writing books like this, students reinforce the language skills in the context of writing. Reading and writing like this weekly, after three or four months most students can use multiple-sentence patterns to talk about their families, schools, communities, and daily life experiences.

Many middle and high school teachers have concerns about using pattern books for fear they are too babyish and their ELL students will be insulted if asked to read and write them. My suggestion for teaching older ELLs is to use pattern books only for language learning and practice, not for learning new concepts or building knowledge.

At a workshop for high school ESL teachers, I asked the audience to learn some Chinese by giving them a short story and a pattern book. I let them read both and asked them to decide which book would be the most helpful. They all responded to the Chinese pattern book. I then asked them if they felt insulted by reading/writing such a simple pattern book. They all said no, and felt proud of themselves for being able not only to say, "I love my mother; I love my father; I love my brother," but also to create many more sentences with the same pattern. I knew if I tried to explain to them what "father" meant and what "love" meant, they would be very insulted. No matter how old the learners are, we should start where they are and make them feel capable of learning and taking risks rather than confusing them, drilling them with language skills in isolation, and disabling them with unmanageable tasks. We would be so proud of ourselves if we could say, "I love you," and "My name is . . ." in multiple

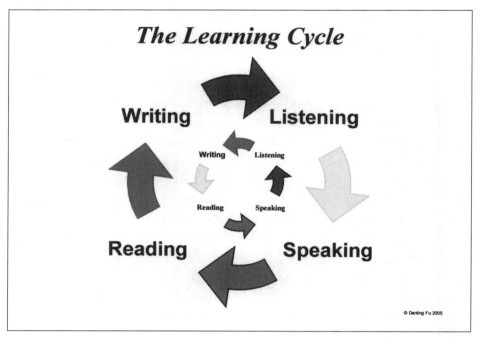

Figure 6.2   *Language Learning Cycle*

languages, and even prouder if we could do so in writing. That is how
beginning ELLs feel when they are learning English. In addition, there
are more and more published pattern books with more age-appropriate
content available for secondary students, such as *The Houses That Jack
Built* by Graham Masterton and *The House That Crack Built* by Clark
Taylor.

For L1 acquisition, the learning cycle starts with listening, then speaking, reading, and writing. But for L2 acquisition, this cycle may start with
writing, especially for older ELL students, as Figure 6.2 indicates (the outside cycle shows L1 learning and the inside L2 learning). As ELLs write,
they can spend more time thinking—searching for words and mentally
translating—whereas when speaking, they are unable to do all these spontaneously. Thus, ELLs are able to say more in writing English than they

can express in English orally. In order to help them speak more often and more proficiently, we can use writing as a springboard to improving oral reading fluency and speaking ability. From their writing, we also learn what language skills they need to write, speak, and read well.

Teaching Vocabulary, Spelling, and Grammar Skills Through Writing

Vocabulary building and spelling practice no doubt are crucial to ELLs' language learning. "Don't know the words" or "Don't have enough vocabulary" are heard most when ELLs express their frustration in reading and writing in English. ESL instructors spend a lot of time and effort building ELLs' vocabulary and spelling skills, but learning vocabulary only from reading and weekly spelling lessons won't help ELLs learn the English language effectively because they can't remember all the new words without using them frequently in a meaningful context.

Vocabulary should be taught to ELLs across subject areas. Teachers who have even one ELL in their classrooms are English language teachers. They need to teach subject content, reading and writing, and language skills systematically integrated with teaching the new knowledge and concepts. ELLs can't develop enough vocabulary just in the ESL or English classrooms because they need to learn new vocabulary and terminology connected with the content they are learning and the texts they are reading in each class or subject area. Since it takes five to seven years to develop academic language skills (Cummins 1981; Thomas and Collier 1997), which are mostly connected with content learning, subject-area teachers should build vocabulary instruction for ELLs into their curriculum. As I discussed in Chapter 5, writing is the best way for ELLs to digest their reading and deepen their knowledge; it is also the best way to practice using language skills through writing.

In our bilingual/social studies class at Dr. Sun Yat Sen Middle School, students are introduced to content-specific English vocabulary through learning subject content in their native language. When they write essays in their native language, they insert the vocabulary introduced in their writing to practice using the learned vocabulary in context. For instance, when they studied the American Civil War, they were introduced to vocabulary listed in Figure 6.3.

Then, in their writing, the students mixed in the English vocabulary they learned to present their understanding of the subject (see Figure 6.4).

Gradually, students in this bilingual social studies class developed their academic vocabulary while learning content knowledge. The academic vocabulary building helped the ELLs tremendously when they later began to study social studies topics in their ESL and English classes.

In ESL class, students were systematically taught English vocabulary, spelling, and grammar through writing. At the beginning, when writing in their daily or weekend journals in their native language, the teachers would

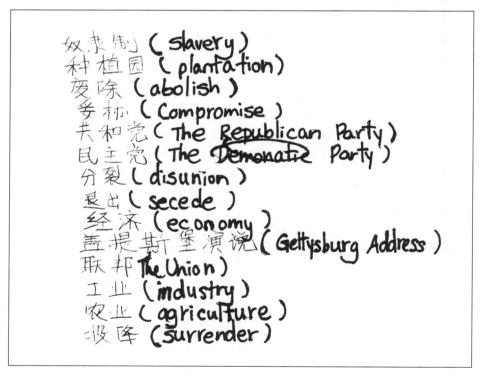

Figure 6.3 *Vocabulary Introduction*

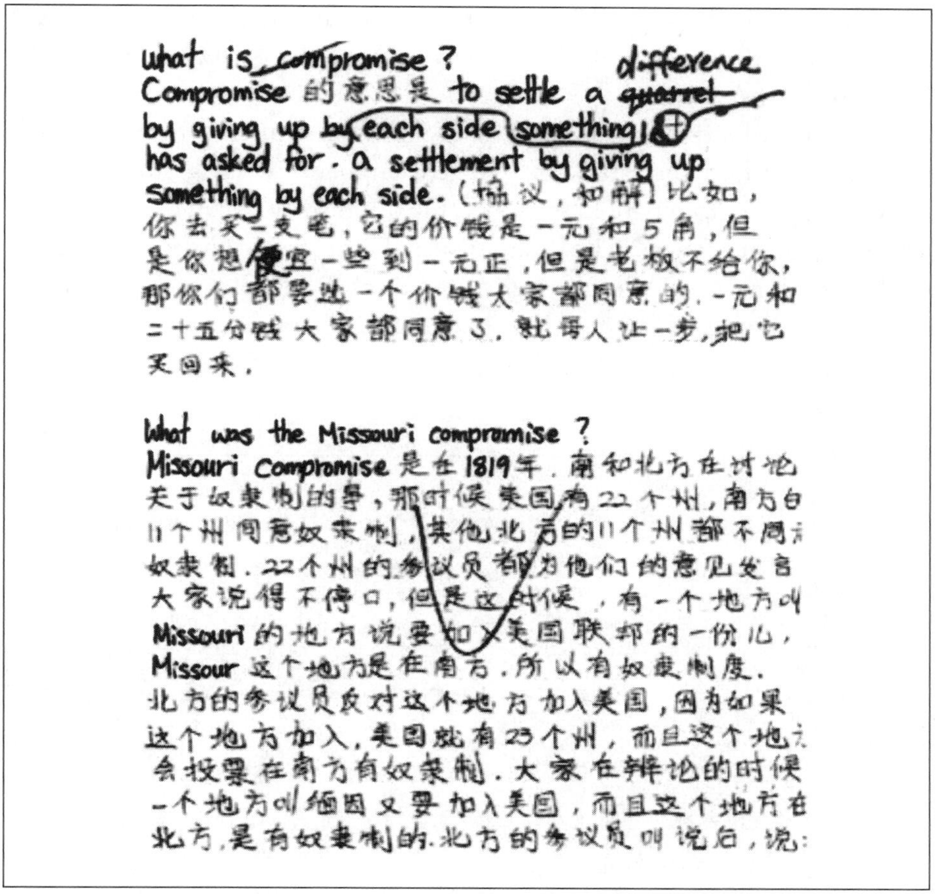

what is compromise?
Compromise 的意思是 to settle a quarrel difference
by giving up by each side something &
has asked for. a settlement by giving up
something by each side. (协议,和解) 比如,
你去买一支笔,它的价钱是一元和5角,但
是你想便宜一些到一元正,但是老板不给你,
那你们都要些一个价钱大家都同意的.一元和
二十五分钱大家都同意了.就得人让一步,把它
买回来.

What was the Missouri compromise?
Missouri Compromise 是在1819年.南和北方在讨地
关于奴隶制的事,那时候美国有22个州,南方的
11个州同意奴隶制,其他北方的11个州都不同意
奴隶制.22个州的参议员都为他们的意见发言
大家说得不停口,但是这时候,有一个地方叫
Missouri 的地方说要加入美国联邦的一份儿,
Missour 这个地方是在南方.所以有奴隶制度.
北方的参议员反对这个地方加入美国,因为如果
这个地方加入,美国就有23个州,而且这个地方
会投票在南方有奴隶制.大家在辩论的时候
一个地方叫缅因又要加入美国,而且这个地方在
北方,是有奴隶制的.北方的参议员叫说白,说:

Figure 6.4   *Work for Social Studies on the Civil War*

choose key words, phrases, and sentence structures from their journal writing as their weekly language learning. These words and phrases were closely connected to the students' daily life: for example, *watch TV; play computer games; have breakfast, lunch, and dinner; school; home; family; after school; play basketball with friends; I go to school or go home; I watch TV with my family; I play basketball with my friends after the school; I do homework before I go to bed*, and so on. From week to week, students learned more English words and phrases that they needed in order to express their life experiences. Each week, they would incorporate these newly learned words into their journal writing. That is why code-switching writing was a common practice among all ELLs shortly after they started writing in the ESL classrooms.

With more and more English language skills taught in the context of their writing, the students' mixed-language writing was at first native-language dominated, then became English dominated with a few native-language words. The examples in Figures 6.5 and 6.6 illustrate a Chinese-dominated piece mixed with English words and an English-dominated writing spotted with a few Chinese characters.

I.S 131
6-617

My thought about the Civil War 四月 19 2000年

我的思想關于 Civil War

如果一個人說美國的北方和南方要有一個戰爭. 一個國家自己部了戰爭， 那戰爭是叫做 Civil War.
Civil War 是一個不好的事情没有人想要有一個 Civil War. 如果一個國家有一個 Civil War. 他們的國家是很凌亂的。他們要损失很多東西他們要毁坏很多城市和很多房子。 Civil War 結束了後在北方和南方死了很多人。以前美國有一個 Civil War 是因爲北方和南方有不同的思想。關于奴隸有不同的思想。北方是不喜歡 slavery。但是南方想有 slavery.南方想有 slavery 因爲南方靠農業去賺錢。北方靠工業去賺錢。在南方需要很多奴隸去耕種作物。但是北方用很多交易買賣。我們要去學怎樣去交易和怎樣去買賣。但是你不要學怎樣去挑一個水果。南方有奴隸那樣我們叫南方奴隸州和我們叫北方自由州。然後北方和南方有一個辩論因爲有一個地方想參加美國。那地方是叫做 Missouri。如果這地方參加美國，美國有23但是美國 will 有12奴隸州。和北方只有11州然後 Maine 參加美國轉了自由州。然後 Lincoln 做美國總統。很多南方人不喜歡 Lincoln，因爲他相信奴隸販子是壞的在那時候很多奴隸離開聯盟。Civil War 開始了。Civil War 打了4年聯盟赢了，南方回去了聯盟。5天後 Lincoln 和他的妻子去看演出一個叫做 Wilkes Booth 暗殺他。當 Lincoln 死了時候美國 pass the 十四修正案，十四修正案說每個人在美國誕生的人是美國公民。十五修正案說如果你是美國公民你有权去投票。那 Civil War 結束美國面對很多問題 1，經濟 2，社會3，政治。

THE END

Figure 6.5 *Chinese-Dominated Mixed-Language Writing*

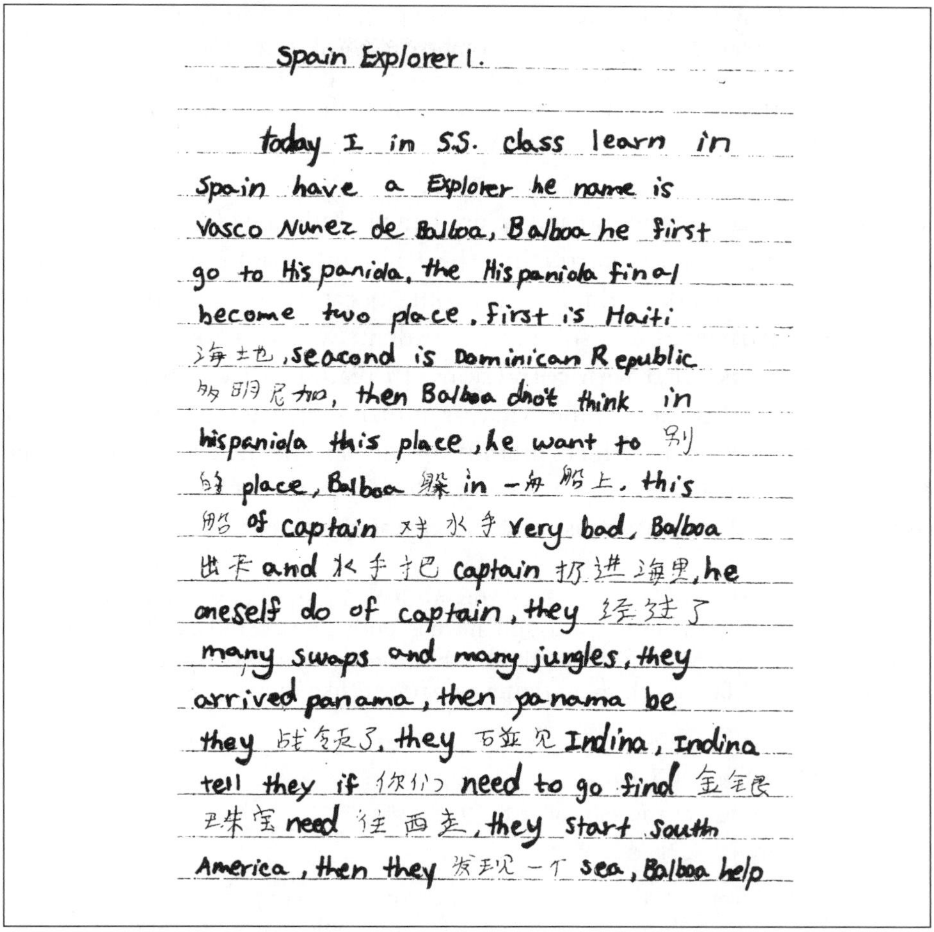

Figure 6.6 *English-Dominated Mixed-Language Writing*

With consistent teaching of vocabulary, spelling, and grammar in the context of the students' writing at the beginning of the year, many ELLs were ready to try their hand at writing entirely in English after the winter break. Their initial attempts were at the inter-language stage, as in the following example:

Today, I 8 o'clock get up. I go to the school, I in the school eat the breakfast. In the CLA the class the Ms L give we are Wednesday the test back. I just 51%. I think is very not good. I think today after the school go to the game store play the video games. Tomorrow I will go to the school study the ESL. And I and Wersua go to the shopping buy the some thing. I go home eat the dinner and watch the TV watch the video and many many thing, I feel tomorrow is very happy.

The writing and sentence structure are heavily influenced by the student's native language. Simply correcting the language wouldn't help the students gain command of English, not only because every sentence would need to be rewritten, but also because students would be overwhelmed by seeing their work filled with corrections. In reading ELLs' inter-language writing, we need to determine what grammar skills they need in order to improve. Betty told us which grammar skills she needed to teach in her ESL class and explained how to teach them in order to help students like the one in the example we just saw to express their daily activities:

> When I read this piece, I could tell this student doesn't know the basic sentence to tell his daily life, though he has enough vocabulary. There are many students who tend to write like this due to their first language influence. I would first teach them sentence patterns like this:
>
> > I get up at 8 o'clock.
> > I go to school at 8:15.
> > I eat breakfast at the school at 8:30.
> > I have my CLA class at 9:00.
>
> I would contrast this sentence structure with what they wrote: "I 8 o'clock get up" to show the difference. Then I would ask the students to use this sentence structure (subject + verb + object + time) to tell what they do every day. Then, I would teach them to expand their sentences:
>
> > I go to school to study English.
> > I go to the store to play video games.
> > I go home to watch TV.
> > I play basketball with my friends after the school.
>
> And gradually I teach them to write complicated sentences like:
>
> > I go to school after I have my breakfast.
> > I play basketball with my friends after I finish my homework.

I cook dinner for the family when I get home.

I help my friends if I can.

I want them to be able to express their daily life experiences in Standard English, so they can communicate with others better. I spend the first two months of the school year teaching my beginner ELLs communicative language.

Betty used her students' daily journal writing to look for the vocabulary words and grammar skills her students needed to learn gradually in order to share their life experiences. She couldn't teach them everything at once because, as she said, "Nobody can learn that way. I teach them gradually, with one or two sentence patterns a week." It is easy for teachers to be shocked to see so many errors in students' inter-language writing, and not to know what grammar skills they should start to teach these students. Betty, too, was shocked before she learned to help her students gain a good sense of English grammar and teach them what they needed slowly and systematically rather than drilling them with grammar skills in isolation. Instead of teaching from sequence-and-scope textbooks, Betty looked for vocabulary words and grammar skills her ELLs actually needed to learn in their writing for her language instruction. Through this relevant instruction, her ELLs slowly learned to write with fewer errors and to make transitions to writing in conventional English.

My suggestions for helping ELLs develop their speaking, reading, and language skills through writing can be summarized as follows:

◆ Let students use writing to prepare their oral presentation.

◆ Use students' own writing for reading practice.

◆ Guide students to write pattern books and practice reading their pattern books and then orally express themselves in simple English.

◆ Look at their writing (in various forms and languages) for what language skills they need in order to communicate well in English and then teach them those skills gradually.

- Prepare them to share their writing (personal narrative and academic writing) in groups and in class.

- Use students' writing as examples to compare and contrast linguistic features of their native language and English.

- Let students self-edit and peer-edit their writing.

- Provide writing opportunities for ELLs in every subject area for their academic language development.

ELLs develop their English proficiency effectively through interrelated writing, reading, listening, and speaking activities that have to happen in every class they take and in every subject they study. Writing incorporates all language skills. Teaching writing is a contextual and meaningful way for ELLs to develop their language proficiency.

Becoming Bilingual Writers

7

This book presents a model for ELLs' transition in their writing development from native language to English. However, I often wonder about this transition myself. I am a fluent bilingual writer with publications in both Chinese and English. When I write, either in my native language or in English, code-switching or inter-language always pops up. My Chinese writing is heavily laced with English expressions, and my English writing is usually flavored with a strong Chinese accent. After living, studying, and teaching in the English-speaking world for over twenty years, sometimes I can't tell which language, Chinese or English, is more native to me. I tend to be more fluent and comfortable engaging in academic discussions and talking about my life experience in the States in English. But Chinese gives me a certain intimacy and familiarity that connects me with my cultural roots. It is like Chinese food to me, without which for a few days, I would not feel my life to be complete. Ulla Connor (1996), a known researcher in composition rhetoric, shares similar thoughts as a bilingual writer:

> Twenty years later, after earning a Ph.D and gaining several years of teaching and research experience in applied linguistics in the United States, I finally think that I am close to the final stage of second language development. This stage allows a learner to let ideas flow on paper without the interference of having to translate them or being overly conscious of the language. With this last stage comes confidence in oneself as a writer in

English. This does not mean, of course, that I am unaware of some nonna-tiveness in my writing. For example, because Finnish uses neither articles nor prepositions, I tend to use them inappropriately. (4)

Similarly, Abby Figueroa (2004), a Spanish-English bilingual author, expresses her thoughts:

> Everything I find myself thinking, speaking, and breaking in two languages though, I disagree with everyone who thinks that speaking both simultane-ously is a disgrace. Well, make that almost two languages. I'm the first to admit that my Spanish isn't perfect. Far from it. But not for a second do I believe that my deliberate Spanglish, my twisting and turning through dos idiomas, is wrong. At the very least it helps me express myself more precisely. A larger vocabulary, dozens more idioms, mas chistes, all this and more makes my world more colorful. Le dam as sabor a mis pensamientos. (284)

Bilinguals' work (speaking and writing) tends to blend the features of two languages/cultures. Much work on bilingual communication has been reported globally. In their study on Turkish-speaking immigrant students in Germany, Dirim and Hieronymus (2003) found that students often code-switched their languages for various communicative purposes and frequently created new language forms that emerged from both German and Turkish—linguistic hybrids—to meet their ends in communication.

Recently, I read some discussions among applied linguists across the world on Standard English varieties. The universally accepted varieties of Standard English are British English, American English, Canadian English, New Zealand English, Australian English, Hong Kong English, and Indian English. An article published in *Changing English*, a U.K. applied linguis-tics journal, advocates an acceptance of China English (Chen and Hu 2006). In this article, the authors discuss the difference between Chinese English/Chinglish and China English. The former is an inter-language (with first-language interference) and the latter is proposed as a variety of Standard English just like Hong Kong English or Australian English. The authors of this article also state:

> According to Hu Xiaoqiong (2004), there is no clear distinction between the two terms; rather they are at the opposite ends of a continuum. At one

end, it is an incorrect form of English. The words are ungrammatically strung together, with often inappropriate lexis and probably only a partially comprehensible pronunciation. On the other end it is a language as good a communicative tool as Standard English. The pronunciation is close enough not to pose much of a problem; there may be some syntactic and grammatical differences attributable to the influence of Chinese; and the lexis may occasionally differ, reflecting cultural differences. (232)

At the opposite end of the continuum from Chinglish, a form of pidgin English (inter-language), is China English, a variety of Standard English discussed by these two linguists to represent the development of ELL writers in becoming bilingual writers. However, most of the studies done on the features of bilingual communication, such as code-switching and inter-language, focus on the oral communication of bilinguals, and fewer focus on their written communications.

As in their oral communication, bilingual writers compose from a bilingual frame of mind and perspective, which distinctly embellishes their writing. This unique "nonnativeness" in the writing of the bi/multilinguals, rather than being termed *fossilized errors* in the ESL field, can be seen as a "hybrid" of literacies demonstrated by bi/multilinguals. Raymond Federman (2003), a French/English novelist, expressed in the following what many bilingual writers claim: that they tend to blend their languages in their composing process:

> I don't seem to feel . . . that there is a space between the two languages in me that keeps them apart. On the contrary, for me French and English always seem to overlap, to want to merge, to want to come together, to want to embrace one another, to mesh one into the other. Or if you prefer, they want to spoil and corrupt one another. Therefore, I do not feel that one language is vertical in me, and the other horizontal, as you suggest. If anything, they seem to be standing or lying in the same direction—sometimes vertically and other times horizontally, depending on their moods or their desires. Though the French and the English in me occasionally compete with one another in some vague region of my brain, more often they play with one another, especially when I put them on paper. Yes, I think that the two languages in me love each other and I have, on occasion, caught them having wild intercourse behind my back. However, I cannot tell you which is feminine and which is masculine, perhaps they are androgynous. (237)

The meshing of two languages described by Federman reveals a linguistic interface in the writing of bilingual writers. I am confident that our ELLs will develop into writers as Raymond Federman describes some day if we respect their bilingual or multilingual mind, hold a developmental perspective toward the transitions they are making in becoming bilingual writers, and show our delight in their unique voice reflected through their flexible using of languages or linguistic hybrid form in their writing. In teaching ELLs to write, we need to see the importance of ELLs' first-language writing skills and value the transitional stages in their learning to write in English. Forcing them to think only in English is to cripple the full extent of their intelligence and neglect all their competencies (or funds of knowledge).

Learning to write in a new language is a lifelong process of transformation because it involves not only learning a new set of language skills and vocabulary, but also constantly forming new ways of thinking and expressing and creating divergent discourse to express bi/multilingual perspectives. Learning to write in English for ELLs who are literate in their native language is actually a process of becoming bilingual writers, rather than merely replacing one language or writing ability with another or mastering two separate language systems. ELLs' native language will always be part of them, their identity, their funds of knowledge, and their tools for thinking and expressing. If writing reflects who and what the writers are, then ELLs' native language (voice and expressions) will either visibly appear (in the mixed-language style) or be blended with English (inter-language) in their writing. Harklau and Pinnow (2009) state that we are in great need of theories of adolescent literacy that take multilingual students as their norm:

> Our dependence on monolingual models of teaching and learning literacy leads us to define L2 writing merely as a problem or L2 deficit, rather than considering writers' entire linguistic repertoires and resources. Nevertheless, multilingual students outnumber monolingual students globally, and adolescent second-language writing research would benefit by paralleling the recent move in the field of second language acquisition toward a model of "multicompetency" (Cook, 2003, Ortega, 2006, Valdes, 1999) that can explore the complex ecology of linguistic and cultural assets that multilingual students bring to composing. (135)

Unfortunately, most ELLs lose their native-language writing competencies after they succeed in becoming proficient writers in English. The major reason for this loss is the lack of practical value in using their native writing in everyday life in the United States. When they are mainstreamed into regular education, they study everything in English. They don't need to write in their native language to function in this English-dominated world. This lack of practical values of ELLs' native language indicates the strong differential in language status between official and subordinate languages that currently exists in the United States, and this often carries direct consequences for speakers of the subordinate languages (Tse 2001).

For new immigrant students, opportunities for educational success, economic advancement, and a sense of self-worth as an "American" must be weighed against keeping open lines of communication with one's immediate or extended family, neighbors, and cultural affiliates. Because the majority of immigrant children come from low-income families, most have little choice but to adopt English as their language of preference if they hope to flourish in this country. Although ELLs may find themselves serving as bilingual translators for their parents, they are not apt to be afforded the opportunity to further develop their native-language skills beyond those required by domestic situations.

The current demand that new immigrant students pass the same standardized tests as their native-English-speaking peers after one year (in Florida) or three years (in New York) in this nation pushes these students into English monolingual status, which results in the ever faster loss of their primary language. Some have argued that these losses are simply the price immigrant families must pay for choosing to live in the United States. However, many believe this high price is not paid by immigrants alone. The negative consequence of language loss and the benefits of continuing the development of ELLs' native-language competence have far-reaching implications for the individual as well as the larger U.S. society (Tse 2001). A lack of foresight with respect to issues relative to the rapid burgeoning of a subordinate-language-speaking population may also be attributed to a set of beliefs that Luis Moll (2001) calls "official nationalism" (13). Bernhardt

(2000) made a particularly salient point about the effects of attitude about bilingual or multilingual language learning:

> In the notoriously monolingual Anglophone world *language* is frequently synonymous with English. . . . This monolingualism, that is English-language monolingualism, is such a dominant dimension in the Anglophone world that it is often difficult to get even the most astute scholar to think about the worlds in ways other than with an Anglophone view. (791)

The idea that the United States must remain monolingual in order to maintain its identity and coherence appears to prevail and is reflected in our educational policies. The fact that over one-half of the world population is bilingual (Kohnert 2004) suggests that bilingualism not only helps serve transitional needs, but that becoming bilingual is not as overwhelmingly difficult or potentially confusing as we might suspect. Further, the fact that the acquisition of a second language has historically been a mark of erudition among the educated elite suggests that, at some level, bilingualism is a socially and culturally desirable goal (Fu and Matoush 2006). Reyes (2001) calls for unleashing possibilities for bilingual children:

> The time has come to consider biliteracy the new threshold for literacy achievement in the new millennium. When this becomes a reality, Latino students and other bilinguals will be repositioned at the center of the curriculum rather than at the margins. To be satisfied with less than this is to accept a lower ceiling for our children's academic achievement and to force them to develop only half their potential. (119)

In the twenty-first century, our world is becoming more globally interdependent. As a nation of immigrants, we should view new immigrants as an asset rather than a liability. Our ELLs are at the forefront of global competency. We should value what they bring with them—including their languages, cultures, and ethnic spirit—as resources (human capital) rather than as barriers to learning or a threat to society. We also should continue to enhance the development of their native-language competence while cultivating their English learning and academic ability in this English-dominated world.

References

Alatis, E. J. 2005. "Kachu's Circles and the Growth of Professionalism in TESOL." *English Today* 82 (21:2): 25–34.

Allington, R. 2005. *What Really Matters to Struggling Readers? Research-Based Reading Programs.* 2nd ed. New York: Longman.

Anzaldua, G. 1987. *Borderland/la frontera: The New nestiza.* San Francisco: Aunt Lute Books.

Applebee, A. H., and J. Langer. 2006. *The State of Writing Instruction in America's Schools: What Existing Data Tell Us.* Center on English Learning and Achievement, University at Albany-State University of New York. www.albany.edu.

August, D., and T. Shanahan. 2006. *Developing Literacy in Second Language Learners: Report of the National Literacy Panel on Language Minority Children and Youth.* Mahwah, NJ: Lawrence Erlbaum.

Bernhardt, E. B. 2000. "Second-Language Reading as a Case Study of Reading Scholarship in the Twentieth Century." In *Handbook of Reading Research 3,* edited by M. Kamil, P. Mosenthal, P. D. Pearson, and B. Barr, 791–811. Mahwah, NJ: Lawrence Erlbaum.

Browning-Aiken, A. 2005. "Border Crossings: Funds of Knowledge Within an Immigrant Household." In *Funds of Knowledge: Theorizing Practice in Households, Communities, and Classrooms,* edited by N. Gonsalez, L. C. Moll, and C. Amanit, 167–81. Mahwah, NJ: Lawrence Erlbaum.

Calkins, L. 1994. *The Art of Teaching Writing.* Portsmouth, NH: Heinemann.

Cammarota, J. 2007. "A Social Justice Approach to Achievement: Guiding Latina/o Students Toward Educational Attainment with a Challenging, Socially Relevant Curriculum." *Equity and Excellence in Education* 40 (1): 87–96.

Carrasquillo, A. & V. Rodriguez. 1995. *Language Minority in the Mainstream Classroom.* Philadelphia, PA: Multilingual Matters Ltd.

Cazden, C., and C. E. Snow. 1990. Pref. to "English Plus: Issues in Bilingual Education." *Annuals of the American Academy of Political and Social Science* 508: 9–11.

Chen, M., and X. Hu. 2006. "Toward the Acceptance of China English at Home and Abroad." *Changing English* 13 (2): 231–40.

Cohen, A., and A. Brooks-Carson. 2001. "Research on Direct Versus Translated Writing: Students' Strategies and Their Results." *The Modern Language Journal* 85 (2): 169–88.

Connor, U. 1996. *Contrastive Rhetoric: Cross-Cultural Aspects of Second-Language Writing*. Cambridge: Cambridge University Press.

Cook, V. 1995. "Multi-Competence and the Learning of Many Languages." *Language, Culture & Communication* 892: 93–98.

———. 2003. *Effects of the Second Language on the First*. Buffalo, NY: Multilingual Matters.

Cummins, J. 1979. *Linguistic Interdependence and the Educational Development of Bilingual Children*. Bilingual Education Paper Series 3/2 (ERIC Document Reproduction Service No. 257312).

———. 1981. "The Role of Primary Language Development in Preventing Educational Success for Language Minority Students." In *Schooling and Language Minority Students: A Theoretical Framework*, edited by the California State Department of Education, 3–49. Los Angeles: California State University, Evaluation, Dissemination and Assessment Center.

Cumming, A. 1987. Decision Making and Text Representation in ESL Writing Performance. Paper presented at the TESOL International Conference, Miami Beach, Florida.

———. 1989. "Writing Expertise and Second Language Proficiency." *Language Learning* 39: 81–141.

———. 1990. "Metalinguistic and Ideational Thinking in Second Language Composing." *Written Communication* 7: 482–511.

Davis, L. H., J. F. Carlistle, and M. Beeman. 1999. "Hispanic Children's Writing in English and Spanish When English Is the Language Instruction." *Yearbook of the National Reading Conference* 48: 238–48.

Dirim, I., and A. Hieronymun. 2003. "Cultural Orientation and Language Use Among Multilingual Youth Groups: 'For me it is like we all speak one language.'" In *Bilingualism & Social Relations: Turkish Speakers in North Western Europe*, edited by J. Norman Jorgensen, 42–55. Buffalo, NY: Multilingual Matters.

Dufva, M., and M. J. M. Voeten. 1999. "Native Language Literacy and Phonological Memory as Prerequisites for Learning English as a Foreign Language." *Applied Psycholinguistics* 20 (3): 329–48.

Durgunoglu, A. Y. 2002. "Cross-Linguistic Transfer in Literacy and Development and Implications for Language Learners." *Annals of Dyslexia* 52: 189–204.

Edelsky, C. 1982. "Writing in a Bilingual Program: The Relation of L1 and L2 Texts." *TESOL Quarterly* 16: 211–28.

Federman, R. 2003. "A Voice Within a Voice: Federman Translating/Translating Federman." In *The Multilingual Mind: Issues Discussed by, for and About People Living with Many Languages*, edited by T. Tokuhama-Espinosa, 235–42. Westport, CT: Praeger.

Figueroa, A. 2004. "Speaking Spanglish." In *Tongue Tied: The Lives of Multilingual Children in Public Education*, edited by Otto S. Ana, 284–86. New York: Rowman & Littlefield.

Freeman, Y., and D. Freeman. 1996. *Teaching Reading and Writing in Spanish in the Bilingual Classroom*. Portsmouth, NH: Heinemann.

———. 2002. *Closing the Achievement Gap: How to Reach Limited-Formal-Schooling and Long-Term English Learners*. Portsmouth, NH: Heinemann.

———. 2005. *Dual Language Essentials*. Portsmouth, NH: Heinemann.

Freire, P. 1970. *Pedagogia del oprimido*. DF, Mexico: Siglo Veintiuno Editores.

Fu, D. 1995. *"My Trouble Is My English": Asian Students and the American Dream*. Portsmouth, NH: Heinemann.

———. 2003. *An Island of English: Teaching ESL in Chinatown*. Portsmouth, NH: Heinemann.

———. 2007a. "A Collaboration Between ESL and Regular Classroom Teachers for ELL Students' Literacy Development." *Changing English* 14 (3): 325–42.

———. 2007b. "Teaching Writing to English Language Learners." In *Teaching the Neglected "R": Rethinking Writing Instruction in Secondary Classrooms*, edited by Thomas Newkirk and Richard Kent, 225–42. Portsmouth, NH: Heinemann.

Fu, D., and M. Matoush. 2006. "Writing Development and Biliteracy." In *The Politics of Second Language Writing*, edited by P. Matsuda, C. Ortmeier-Hooper, and X. You, 5–29. West Lafayette, IN: Parlor Press.

Fu, D., and J. Townsend. 1998. "Cross-Cultural Dilemmas in Writing: The Need for Transformation of Teaching and Learning." *College Teaching* 46 (4): 128–33.

Garcia, E. E. 2001. *Hispanic Education in the United States: Raices alas*. New York: Rowman & Littlefield.

Garcia, O. 2002. "Writing Backwards Across Languages: The Inexpert English/Spanish Biliteracy of Uncertified Bilingual Teachers." In *Developing Advanced Literacy in First and Second Languages: Meaning with Power*, edited by M. J. Schleppegrell and M. C. Colombi, 245–60. New York: Routledge.

Genesse, F., K. Lindholm-Leary, W. Saunders, and D. Christian. 2005. "English Language Learners in U.S. Schools: An Overview of Research Findings." *Journal of Education for Students Placed at Risk* 10: 363–85.

Gibbons, P. 2002. *Scaffolding Language, Scaffolding Learning: Teaching Second Language Learners in the Mainstream Classroom*. Portsmouth, NH: Heinemann.

Graves, D. 1983. *On Writing: Teachers and Children at Work*. Portsmouth, NH: Heinemann.

Grosjean, F. 1989. "Neurolinguistics, Beware! The Bilingual Is Not Two Monolinguals in One Person." *Brain & Language* 36: 3–15. *The Encyclopedia of Language and Linguistics*. 1994. Oxford: Pergamon Press.

Hansen, J. 1987. *When Writers Read*. Portsmouth, NH: Heinemann.

Harklau, L., and R. Pinnow. 2009. "Adolescent Second-Language Writing." In *Handbook of Adolescent Literacy Research*, edited by L. Christenbury, R. Bomer, and P. Smagorinsky, 126–39. New York: The Guilford Press.

Hillocks, G. 1995. *Teaching Writing as Reflective Practice*. New York: Teachers College Press.

Hruska, B. 2000. Prioritizing Needs/Negotiating Practices: Student Placement at River Valley Elementary. Paper presented at the Puerto Rican Studies Association Conference, Amherst, Massachusetts, October 28. Retrieved on 8/28/05 at www.eric.ed.gov/ERICWebPortal/Home.portal.

Hu, X. Q. 2004. "Why China English Should Stand Alongside British, American, and the Other 'World Englishes.'" *English* Today 78 (20.2): 26–33.

Hudelson, S. 1986. "ESL Children's Writing: What We've Learned, What We're Learning." In *Children and ESL: Integrating Perspectives*, edited by P. Rigg and D. S. Enright, 25–54. Alexandria, VA: Teachers of English to Speakers of Other Languages.

Hudson, P., and S. Fradd. 1990. "Cooperative Planning for Learners with Limited English Proficiency." *Teaching Exceptional Children* 23 (1): 16–21.

Hurren, P. 1993. "Expanding the Collaborative Planning Model to Meet the Needs of ESL Students." *Emergency Librarian* 20 (5). Retrieved on 8/9/05 at http://bll.epnet.com.lp.hcsl.ufl.edu/.

Kohn, A. 2006. *The Homework Myth*. Cambridge, MA: Da Capo Lifelong Books.

Kohnert, K. 2004. "Processing Skills in Early Sequential Bilingual." In *Bilingual Language Development and Disorders in Spanish-English Speakers*, edited by B. A. Goldstein, 77–104. Baltimore, MD: Paul H. Brookes.

Laman, T. T., and K. V. Sluys. 2008. "Being and Becoming: Multilingual Writers' Practices." *Language Arts* 85 (4): 265–74.

Lanauze, M., and C. E. Snow. 1989. "The Relation Between First- and Second-Language Writing Skills: Evidence from Puerto Rican Elementary School Children in Bilingual Programs." *Linguistics and Education* 1 (4): 323–39.

Larios, J. R., J. Marin, and L. Murphy. 2001. "A Temporal Analysis of Formulation Processes in L1 and L2 Writing." *Language Learning* 51 (3): 497–538.

Leki, I. 1991. "Twenty-Five Years of Contrastive Rhetoric: Text Analysis and Writing Pedagogies." *TESOL Quarterly* 25 (1): 123–43.

Liebscher, G., and J. Dailey-O'Cain. 2005. "Learning Code-Switching in the Content-Based Foreign Language Classroom." *The Modern Language Journal* 89 (2): 234–47.

Liu, Y. 2004. The Cognitive Process of Translation in L2 Writing. Ph.D. diss., Indiana University. Retrieved May 23, 2008, from *Dissertation & Thesis: Full Text Database*. (Publication No. AAT3166666).

Lumme, K., and J. E. Lehto. 2002. "Sixth Grade Pupils' Phonological Processing and School Achievement in a Second and the Native Language." *Scandinavian Journal of Education Research* 46 (2): 207–17.

Martinez-Roldan, C. M., and M. E. Franquiz. 2009. "Latina/o Youth Literacies: Hidden Funds of Knowledge." In *Handbook of Adolescent Literacy Research*, edited by L. Christenbury, R. Bomer, P. Smagorinsky, 323–42. New York: Guilford Press.

Matoush, M., and D. Fu. 2009. "The Paradoxical Situation Created by Test-Driven Schooling for Multilingual Children." In *What the Federal Government Won't Let You Know About Teaching Reading*, edited S. Kucer, 176–97. Urbana, IL: NCTE.

Mercado, C. 2003. "Biliteracy Development Among Latino Youth in New York City Communities: An Unexploited Potential." In *An Ecological Framework for Educational Policy, Research, and Practice in Multilingual Settings*, edited by N. Hornberger, 166–86. Buffalo, NY: Multilingual Matters.

———. 2005. "Seeing What's There: Language and Literacy Funds of Knowledge in New York Puerto Rican Homes." In *Building on Strength: Language and Literacy in Latino Families and Communities*, edited by N. Gonzalez, L. C. Moll, and C. Amanti, 134–47. New York: Teachers College Press.

Moe, E. B., K. M. Ciechanowski, K. Kramer, L. Ellis, R. Carrillo, and T. Collazo. 2004. "Working Toward Third Space in Content Area Literacy: An Examination of Everyday Funds of Knowledge and Discourse." *Reading Research Quarterly* 39: 38–70.

Moll, L. C. 2001. "The Diversity of Schooling: A Cultural-Historical Approach." In *The Best for Our Children: Critical Perspectives on Literacy for Latina Students*, edited by M. Reyes and J. H. Halcon, 3–28. New York: Teachers College Press.

———. 2004. Research on Bilingual Education. Presentation at NCTE in New York City on November, 20.

Moll, L. C., C. Amanti, D. Neff, and N. Gonzalez. 1992. "Funds of Knowledge for Teaching: Using a Qualitative Approach to Connect Homes and Classrooms." *Theory and Practice* 31: 132–41.

Morage e Silva, M. 1988. "Is the Process of Composing in a Second Language Similar to Composing in the First?" *Texas Papers in Foreign Language Education* 1: 16–25.

New, L. 1993. "Sharing the Wealth: The Collaboration of ESL and Mainstream Teachers." *Idiom* 23 (3): 1–5.

Newkirk, T., and R. Kent. 2007. *Teaching the Neglected "R": Rethinking Writing Instruction in Secondary Classrooms.* Portsmouth, NH: Heinemann.

Ortega, L. 2006. Multicompetence, Social Context, and L2 Writing Research Praxis. Paper presented at the symposium on Second Language Writing, Purdue University, Lafayette, IN.

Penfield, J. 1987. "ESL: The Regular Classroom Teacher's Perspective." *TESOL Quarterly* 21 (1): 21–39.

Peregoy, S., and O. Boyle. 2005. *Reading, Writing and Learning in ESL*. New York: Pearson-Allyn and Bacon.

Poplack, S. 1980. "Sometimes I'll Start a Sentence in English y termino en espanol." *Linguistics* 18: 581–616.

Qi, D. S. 1998. "An Inquiry into Language-Switching in Second Language Composing Processes." *Canadian Modern Language Review* 54 (3): 413–35.

Raimes, A. 1991. "Instructional Balance: From Theories to Practices in the Teaching of Writing." In *Linguistics and Language Pedagogy: Georgetown University Round Tale on Language and Lnguistics*, edited by J. E. Alatis, 238–49. Washington, DC: Georgetown University Press.

Reyes, M. 2001. "Unleashing Possibilities: Bilteracy in the Primary Grades." In *The Best for Our Children: Critical Perspectives on Literacy for Latino Students*, edited by M. Reyes and J. H. Halcon, 96–121. New York: Teachers College Press.

Roessingh, H. 2004. "Effective High School ESL Programs: A Synthesis and Meta-analysis." *The Canadian Modern Language Review* 60 (5): 611–36.

Ruiz-de-Velasco, J., and M. Fix. 2000. *Overlooked and Underserved Immigrant Students in U.S. Secondary Schools*. Washington, DC: Center for Applied Linguistics and Andrew W. Mellon Foundation, New York.

Samway, K. D. 2006. *When English Language Learners Write*. Portsmouth, NH: Heinemann.

Schnorr, R. F., and L. Davern. 2005. "Creating Exemplary Literacy Classrooms Through the Power of Teaming." *The Reading Teacher* 58 (6): 494.

Sizer, T. 1991. "No Pain, No Gain." *Educational Leadership* (May): 32–34.

Snelling, P., and A. Van Gelderen. 2004. "The Effect of Enhanced Lexical Retrieval on Second Language Writing: A Classroom Experiment." *Applied Linguistics* 25: 172–200.

TESOL. 2006. *PreK-12 English Language Proficiency Standards*. Alexandria, VA: TESOL.

Thomas, W. P., and V. Collier. 1997. *School Effective for Language Minority Students; NCBE Resource Collection Series No. 9*. Washington, DC: National Clearinghouse for Bilingual Education.

Tse, L. 2001. *Why Don't They Learn English? Separating Fact from Fallacy in the U.S. Language Debate*. New York: Teachers College Press.

Urban Institute. 2005. High Concentration of Limited-English Students Challenges Implementation of No Child Left Behind Act. www.urban.org/url.cfm?ID=9000884.

U.S. Census Bureau. 2003. http://usgovinfo.about.com/cs/censusstatistic/a/latestpopcounts.htm.

Uzawa, K. 1996. "Second Language Learners' Process of L1 Writing, L2 Writing, and Translation from L1 into L2." *Journal of Second Language Writing* 5 (3): 271–94.

Uzawa, K., and A. Cumming. 1989. "Writing Strategies in Japanese as a Foreign Language: Lowering or Keeping Up the Standards." *The Canadian Modern Language Review* 46: 178–94.

Valdes, G. 1999. "Incipient Bilingualism and the Development of English Language Writing Abilities in the Secondary School." In *So Much to Say: Adolescent, Bilingualism, and ESL in the Secondary School*, edited by C. Faltis and P. Wolfe, 138–75. New York: Teachers College Press.

Walqui, A. 2006. "Scaffolding Instruction for English Language Learners: A Conceptual Framework." *The International Journal of Bilingual Education and Bilingualis* 9 (2): 159–80.

Wang, W., and Q. Wen. 2002. "L1 Use in the L2 Composing Process: An Exploratory Study of 16 Chinese EFL Writers." *Journal of Second Language Writing* 11: 225–46.

Woodall, B. R. 2002. "Language-Switching: Using the First Language While Writing in a Second Language." *Journal of Second Language Writing* 11: 7–28.

Yancey, K. B. 2009. "The Impulse to Compose and the Age of Composition." *Research in the Teaching of English* 43 (3): 316–38.

Children's Books

Wordless Books

Anno's Flea Market by Mitsumasa Anno. Penguin Putnam Books for Young Readers (1984).

The Gift by John Prater. Puffin Picture (1987).

The Invitation by Gabriel Lisowski. Henry Holt (March 1980).

Window by Jeannie Baker. Harper/Collins Children's Books (1991).

Pattern Books

Brown Bear, Brown Bear, What Do You See? by Bill Martin Jr. and illustrated by Eric Carle. Henry Holt (1996).

The House That Crack Built by Clark Taylor and illustrated by Jan Thompson Dicks. Chronicle Books (1992).

The Houses That Jack Built by Graham Masterton. Leisure Books (2000).

Study Guide

This study guide is intended to help guide a discussion of the reading, not to check comprehension. Through conversations we share our understanding of the reading and enrich each other's ideas. In these conversations, you can clarify your reading of the chapters, connect the reading with your personal experience as a learner, challenge the author's positions and recommendations, and reflect on your own practice. While there are many ways to structure a study group, it is important to foster a climate in which readers feel free and safe to participate in ongoing conversations and the exchange of ideas. Guidelines can make book study more productive. Here are a few things you might consider:

◆ **Watch group size.** Often the optimal number is four or five to ensure there is time for all to exchange ideas. The larger group can reassemble at the end to debrief.

◆ **Form a group with members with diverse backgrounds and balance the group with different abilities.** Readers with different learning, teaching, linguistic, cultural, or social backgrounds can offer rich and different perspectives in reading discussion. We each bring a personal text to a shared text when we read, and together we can create another text through our discussion.

◆ **Time management.** Make sure every member gets equal time to speak and that everyone has a chance to express her/his opinion. No one person should be dominant or put on the margin silently. Someone in the group should be selected to manage the time.

◆ **Stay focused on the topic.** It is easy to drift from the focus of a reading discussion. A group leader should be chosen to keep the conversation on track.

◆ **Celebrate learning.** Everyone is a learner in the book discussion; nobody is an expert or knows better than the others. Make sure you take time to enjoy one another and celebrate your learning.

The following questions relate to the content in each chapter and offer suggestions, concepts, and ideas for discussion. Enjoy!

Chapter 1: My Decade's Work with ELLs

1. Who is the audience for this book?

2. In what way does this book contribute to the teaching of ELLs and research on ELLs?

3. In what way does this chapter remind you of your own experience in learning to write in a second language?

4. What is the author's experience working in schools? How does this experience help the author understand ELLs?

5. How many different types of ELLs does the author discuss? How are they served in U.S. public schools?

Chapter 2: ELLs' Writing Development

1. Have you been taught to write in a language other than your native one? If so, how would you describe your experience? If not, please interview an ELL about his/her experience with learning to write in English.

2. What is the relationship between first-language literacy and second-language learning? Have you noticed the difference in learning between an ELL with strong first-language literacy and an ELL with weak first-language literacy?

3. How do Xuhua's writing samples help you understand the four stages of ELLs' writing development defined in this chapter?

4. In what way does the author's definition of writing stages differ from that of others?

5. What is your response to the author's definition of ELLs' writing stages?

Chapter 3: Native Language Writing in ELLs' Writing Development

1. What is the role of first language in ELLs learning to write in English?

2. Reflect on your own experience of writing in a new language (if you have any). Did you think or draft in your first language?

3. Try to compose something in a foreign language you have learned.

   a. For your first try, use *only* your second language: don't allow yourself to use your first language to think.

   b. For your second try, write a story using your first language to draft, and then translate it into your second language.

   c. Analyze the writing process, your feelings, and products of these two experiments.

4. What is the importance of letting ELLs write in their first language while learning English?

5. Do you think that ELLs have to develop their English oral language proficiency before they learn to write in English? Explain.

6. What is the relationship between content area reading and writing?

7. What have you learned about the ELLs by reading the (translated) work they did in their native language? Does this understanding of their L1 writing and literacy ability help you to teach them better?

8. What suggestions does the author give for working with the ELLs who are not able to read and write in their first language?

9. How does the author propose that teachers who don't understand their ELLs' first languages teach them to write, try to understand their work, confer with them about their writing, include them in every component of a writing workshop, and assess their work and progress as writers?

10. What challenges could teachers face in teaching ELLs to write following the author's recommendations? What is your position in teaching ELLs in the No Child Left Behind era?

Chapter 4: Transitional Stages in ELLs' Writing Development

1. What is code-switching? Do you use code-switching? If so, under what circumstances?

2. Usually when people talk about code-switching, it is a phenomenon in the oral language of a bilingual or multilingual person. Have you read any study or discussion about code-switching in written language? If so, do you recall any examples?

3. What do you think of allowing ELLs to code-switch in their writing?

4. Are there any advantages to allowing ELLs to use code-switching in their writing? Are there any disadvantages?

5. What is your view of inter-language: is it first language interference or a natural stage of language development for ELLs?

6. What suggestions does the author give in helping ELLs move from the inter-language stage to standard English?

7. In what way do the examples of the two beginning ELLs' work help you understand their progress in learning to write in English?

8. What did their teachers do to enable these two ELLs to make steady progress as writers and English language learners?

9. If possible, please track two ELLs with different native language backgrounds to understand their development as writers in English.

10. What is the difference between the ESL teacher Betty and bilingual teachers in their approaches to helping ELLs to develop as writers and language learners?

11. What does "nonlinear progress in ELLs' writing development" mean?

12. How does the author recommend assessing the ELLs' writing development as they move back and forth between the four writing stages?

Chapter 5: Teaching ELLs to Write

1. What is the primary challenge secondary teachers encounter in teaching ELLs to write in English?

2. What is the connection between reading and writing in content-area learning for ELLs?

3. What would be a solution when textbooks used at the secondary level are too difficult for ELLs to comprehend?

4. As an experiment, try to use multiple books in teaching a social studies topic as the author suggests rather than using just one textbook.

5. What other genre of writing (besides essay type) should secondary ELLs engage in?

6. When we require students to write frequently we need to read their work frequently. What are the author's suggestions to make our work manageable?

7. How can we help ELLs to improve without correcting every error they make in their writing?

8. Give an example to explain the statement: "Teach writers before teaching writing."

9. Why is it important for ESL and regular classroom teachers to collaborate in teaching ELLs?

10. What are the models of ESL programs? What are their advantages and disadvantages based on your own experience?

11. What made Amy and Renee's collaboration work for their ELLs?

12. Is it possible for you to collaborate with other teachers in your school as Amy and Renee did? What support would you need from your school administrators?

13. What do you think were important factors that enabled Xuhua's progress as a writer and language learner within a year?

Chapter 6: Language Instruction Through Writing

1. Describe how to teach speaking skills, reading skills, and other language skills through writing as recommended by the author.

2. Try teaching language skills—grammar, vocabulary, spelling, word choice, and oral language communication—through writing with your own students. Share the results of your work.

3. Search for wordless books with topics that are age-appropriate for your students.

4. Try to use pattern books to learn a new language yourself and see how you feel as a language learner.

5. How does the language learning cycle for ELLs differ from that for native children?

6. What should we look for in ELLs' writing to learn the language skills they need?

7. How did Betty, the ESL teacher, systematically teach her ELLs language skills based the students' work rather than on textbooks?

8. What concepts from this chapter do you think could be applicable to your teaching?

Chapter 7: Becoming Bilingual Writers

1. What is your understanding of ELLs becoming bilingual writers when they are learning to write in English?

2. Discuss these terms: *monolingualism, anglophone worldview, multilingualism,* and *multicompetency.*

3. What do you think ELLs bring to our classrooms as resources for our curriculum?

4. In what way might this book help you change your teaching to unleash the potential of your bilingual students?

Index

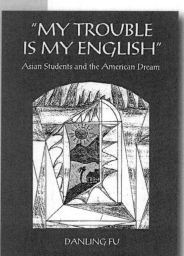